Mark Isaac-Williams was born in Hong Kong in 1939 and was evacuated to Australia with his mother as the threat of Japanese invasion grew. His father was a ship's captain in the Chinese Maritime Customs Service and became a prisoner of war. Returning to Hong Kong at the age of seven, Mark has remained here most of his life. Immediately after the war, his family was billeted for five years in the Peninsula Hotel. It had just been vacated by the Japanese Imperial Forces and was in a terrible condition. Kowloon was then still being developed and together with the hotel it offered Mark an extraordinary playground for adventure. After secondary education in the United Kingdom, Mark began work with the Hong Kong government. He later obtained a degree in botany and specialised in the conservation of wild orchids, joining the Kadoorie Farm and Botanic Garden in 1979. He followed this with his own horticultural and flower shop businesses. He also became a keen philatelist. In the early 2000s, Mark trained as a botanical artist, recording wild orchids in watercolours. He later returned to Kadoorie Farm, where until recently he worked part-time as the Artist in Residence.

The idea for this book was in part conceived from his artistry of the natural world and from his dismay at seeing so many everyday sights from his childhood gradually disappear in the race to build bigger and better without them being comprehensively documented. His was a childhood enjoyed at a unique period in Hong Kong's history and his recording of it in this way is an important contribution to the understanding of the territory's life in the mid-twentieth century.

作者Mark生於1939年的香港，日軍侵略威脅日增，他與母親被逼撤離到澳洲。Mark的父親是一位任職於中國海事海關的船長，戰時淪為階下囚。Mark自七歲時回到香港，大半生定居於此。由於來自公務員家庭，他和家人戰後曾被安排居於半島酒店達五年之久。淪陷時日本皇軍佔據了該酒店，被弄得殘破不堪。戰後正在重建的九龍和半島酒店變成了Mark的歷險樂園。中學負笈英國，畢業後回港投身於政府部門工作，其後修畢植物學學位。他於1979年加入嘉道理農場暨植物園，致力保育野生蘭花；並因此衍生出他的園藝花店生意。他同時也是一名集郵發燒友。2000年代，Mark受訓成為一位植物藝術家，以水彩畫展現野生蘭花的美態；及後重返嘉道理農場，以業餘藝術家身份駐場工作。

這本書的概念源於他對自然世界的藝術觸覺，同時亦有感於童年時每天見到的景物，終不敵與社會發展規律的競賽，逐漸消失於歷史之中，如不及時將它們全面地記錄下來，將有所遺憾。Mark的童年身處於香港歷史中的獨特年代，以這種方式去記錄及刻劃出這個地方二十世紀中葉的風貌，也算是對她的回饋。

"Memories become more precious as we grow older. Our parents did take pictures of us growing up – not many, and I wish there were more. There was me on the swing in a small Tsim Sha Tsui playground with the Peninsula Hotel faintly in the background. There was me eating Dairy Farm ice cream with my brother on a rickshaw by the ferry terminal… and there were us siblings, with all our cousins, wearing our best New Year clothes, playing with firecrackers while our great-grandmother sat on a large rattan chair in her tiny bound feet, clapping and cheering us on…

We grew up on Boundary Street in Kowloon, and tofu fa (sweet beancurd) is still my favourite dessert today. When I finished reading *The Hong Kong I Knew*, my immediate desire was to read it all over again. Mark Isaac-Williams is a remarkable author. Thank you for the wonderful trip down memory lane!"

— Mei Ling Ng, author, Diamond Matchmaker and Charter President, Rotary Club of Homantin Hill

"*The Hong Kong I Knew* captures all the glory and quirkiness of a burgeoning east-meets-west colony at mid-century. Fizzing firecrackers, rickshaws in the rain, balusters of bamboo scaffolding – the charming illustrations and commentary are sure to inspire fond nostalgia for a bygone time."

— Claire Chao, author of *Remembering Shanghai: A Memoir of Socialites, Scholars and Scoundrels*

"Mark Isaac-Williams's *The Hong Kong I Knew* is a fascinating memoir of a lost time and place, the world of the Europeans in Asia in the 1930s, 40s and 50s. Informative, charming and engaging, and written with a real love of Hong Kong and a keen eye, the author's very particular and often quirky choices of topic and viewpoint (not least in his Sights and Scenes of Everyday Life) leave one with wonderfully clear images and feelings, ones which are also very evocative for me – my first experience of Hong Kong was as a very small boy in 1954."

— George Goulding, translator of a number of Nordic Noir and other Swedish authors

"Mark Isaac-Williams brings the reader back to his Kowloon childhood in this delightful story of adventure and change. Growing up mainly at the Peninsula Hotel, he and his friends sometimes got up to mischief by "borrowing" rickshaws or spending days with a visiting circus. These were the years when Hong Kong was rebuilding after WWII and absorbing millions of refugees from over the border, transforming a sleepy colonial outpost into one of the world's most modern cities. And Isaac-Williams was witness to it all. Accompanied by gorgeous illustrations of bygone Hong Kong customs like removing coffins from homes on bamboo slides and transporting cars in ferries across the harbour, *The Hong Kong I Knew* records a Kowloon that has all but disappeared in the name of "progress".

— Susan Blumberg-Kason, author of *Good Chinese Wife: A Love Affair with China Gone Wrong*

"Mark Isaac-Williams's memoir of his childhood records Hong Kong as he knew it in the post-war years. Full of the colours and smells – and variety – of the territory at the time, it is a story that I can commend to all who love Hong Kong. I have vivid memories of Mark cherishing the orchids at Orchid Haven at KFBG. The same passion permeates this book. It is a good read!"

— Dan Bradshaw, WWF-Hong Kong and Kadoorie Farm & Botanic Garden

"Mark's memories of 'old Hong Kong' are a delightful and insightful glimpse of a time long past, in a rapidly changing part of the world. Anyone who lives, or has ever lived, in Hong Kong has a part of their heart here and will not be able to ignore the nostalgic tug that this account evokes – notwithstanding the challenges endured by the former colony and its inhabitants. Even for readers unfamiliar with Hong Kong, there is a taste here of the magic that once was and the spirit that endures through remembrance, all nicely captured by the author."

— Andrew McAulay, Chairperson, Kadoorie Farm & Botanic Garden

THE HONG KONG I KNEW

我認識的香港

SCENES AND STORIES FROM A CHILDHOOD IN KOWLOON

孩童時代於九龍的景物與軼事

Mark Isaac Williams

ILLUSTRATED BY LUCY PARRIS

Lucy Parris 繪圖

BLACKSMITH BOOKS

To all the friends who made life such fun at the time, and especially my best friend D.M.
送給那些年令我人生充滿樂趣的朋友，尤其我的摯友 D.M.

THE HONG KONG I KNEW 我認識的香港
ISBN 978-988-79639-5-0

Copyright © 2021 Mark Isaac-Williams

Published by Blacksmith Books
Unit 26, 19/F, Block B, Wah Lok Industrial Centre,
37-41 Shan Mei Street, Fo Tan, Hong Kong
Tel: (+852) 2877 7899
www.blacksmithbooks.com

First printing 2021

By the same author – 作者其它著作
An Introduction to the Orchids of Asia
The History of the Hong Kong Post Office 1841-1991
Hong Kong Stamps, 1995
Growing Successful Orchids in the Greenhouse and Conservatory
From Dragon to Dragon
Contributor to *The Wild Orchids of Hong Kong*

CONTENTS
內容

Hongkong Bank – 匯豐銀行

Preface

序

Hong Kong is constantly changing. It is its ability to adapt which has enabled it to survive and prosper and yet to remain at heart, the Hong Kong we all cherish. I have lived here a long time and although I find much around me that is still familiar from my childhood, when I stop and truly look back I recognise how much that was once so commonplace, is now disappearing or has already gone forever. This is not only so of its buildings but also of its traditions.

My purpose in writing this book is to record those traditions which have already been lost so that the next generation and those to follow can have an understanding of what Hong Kong was like in the days of their own parents and grandparents. In doing so, and with the help of friends, I have gathered together within these pages as many of the old Chinese customs from Hong Kong's streets, green spaces and waterways as I could remember.

天恆健，自強不息，香港也不例外；不斷的變，是她賴以生存及繁榮之道，這便是我們心繫及珍愛的香港。居港大半生，每當我佇足街頭，回首前塵，身邊景物雖似曾相識，惟不管建築物或一些傳統風貌，都在蛻變或消失於時空中。

滄海桑田，物換星移，傳統事物亦逐漸湮沒於時間的洪流中。為免我們的下一代對父執輩時候的香港感到陌生，在朋友的協助下，我把仍殘留腦海中的回憶整理和記錄下來，從昔日香港的街道，綠化地方以至大溝渠等，儘量勾劃出一些古老的中國傳統，讓它躍然於紙上，好讓下一代能緬懷及認識過去的香港，這是我出版這書的目的。

Mark Isaac-Williams

The Peninsula – 半島酒店

My Story

I was born in Hong Kong in the month of November 1939 in the maternity block of the Kowloon Hospital on Argyle Street. This was just after the start of the Second World War in Europe. My parents were then living in Hong Kong because the Chinese Maritime Customs Service, for which my father worked, had moved its headquarters to Hong Kong from Shanghai after the fall of the city to the Japanese.

In the early 1930s, Britain had been in the grip of the Great Depression. My father had passed his final master's certificate exams in Cardiff, South Wales, in 1934, but could not find permanent work in the British Merchant Navy. In 1935, he was offered a job as Second Mate on a ship going to Shanghai, with the understanding that he could return to Britain with the ship or stay in Shanghai and join the Chinese Maritime Customs Service. He telephoned my mother, whom he had recently met, who agreed that he should stay in Shanghai with a definite job and not to return to uncertainty.

He said he would go if she would promise to join him later to be married there, and this she did, sailing from Southampton on a Japanese ship, the *Yasakuri Maru*, and arriving in Shanghai on 9th October 1936. They were married the next day on the Double Tenth (the anniversary of the Foundation of the Republic of China) at the Holy Trinity Cathedral because it was a holiday and the only time my father was able to get off. My poor mother knew no one at her wedding, not even her matrons of honour. The reception was held at the Cathay Hotel (now the Peace Hotel).

After arriving in Shanghai from Wales, my father had joined the Chinese Maritime Customs on 19th January 1936 and signed a contract for three years; but this was soon cancelled as he was promoted to Acting First Officer and put on the permanent staff. He greatly enjoyed his work in the Customs, which was unique in many ways and had no parallel anywhere in the world.

It had begun very modestly in 1854 during the Qing dynasty as the Imperial Chinese Maritime Customs Service to deal with the tax-collection problems arising from the disturbed conditions caused by the Taiping Rebellion, and eventually became the foremost revenue collector in China. Interestingly, although the Customs was controlled by the Chinese central government throughout its history, it was headed by an Englishman, Sir Robert Hart, and largely staffed at senior levels by foreigners. Its main role was to

我的軼事

我生於一九三九年十一月，二次大戰在歐洲爆發不久，地點就在亞皆老街九龍醫院的產房。隨着日軍攻陷上海，父親工作的中國海事海關總部從上海遷到香港，父母親也因此在這裡住了下來。

上世紀三十年代初，英國正值大蕭條。一九三四年，父親通過他在南威爾斯卡迪夫的碩士課程考試，但卻未能在英國商船公司謀得一職。一九三五年，有船公司給予父親工作，就在一艘開往上海的船上當二副；彼此有一共識，父親可選擇隨船返回英國或留在上海的中國海事海關工作。父親致電母親 — 他剛認識的女友，她同意父親應留在上海，有一份固定工作總比回去人浮於事好。

他對母親說成行與否，取決於她是否答應到上海，跟他重聚並共諧連理。一九三六年，母親乘坐日本輪船藥久丸號，從南安普敦出發，十月九日到達上海。抵埗翌日即在聖三一教堂舉行婚禮，這天剛好是中華民國成立週年的雙十節，也是父親難得的一天假期。結婚酒會設於國泰酒店（即今天的和平飯店），可憐的母親對出席的人無一認識，就是伴娘也不例外。

一九三六年一月十九日，父親剛從威爾斯抵達上海。隨即加入中國海事海關工作，簽約三年。但不多久，合約即取消，父親獲擢升為署任大副，成為永久僱員。他十分享受海關的工作，覺得其獨特之處，世上許多國家都無出其右。

中國帝國海事海關成立於一八五四年的清朝，作為滿清帝國的海事海關，處理因太平天國之亂所引起的稅收問題，最終它成為中國最重要的收入來源。有趣的是，海關雖一直由中國中央政府控制，但掌舵人竟是一位英國人羅拔赫特爵士；而大部份身居高位的都是外國人。海關的主要角色是要準確評估出入口關稅，但時間日久，它的職責也包括在海岸及水道興建燈塔，勘探河道海岸，收取本地河道費用如外灘，橋樑，河流和碼頭的費用，以及報告天氣，打擊走私和防止船隻上發生傳染病。開時負責創建貿易統計及貿易報表，以及上百項的商品專著，如絲綢，皮革，人參，茶葉以至鴉片。它亦協助中國參加差不多三十個國際展覽會，充當中國與外國代表的非式式中介，指導中國訓練她的第一個外交人員，為中國的使館及外交服務奠下基礎。海關的最後一項任務就是承擔郵政服務的行政管理，使它財務運作穩健，直至一九一一年歸入郵電局管轄。

難怪父親說他的生活充滿樂趣。

一九三七年十二月，日本侵華，南京淪陷，也是抗日戰爭中最悲慘的一頁。父親接到命令乘船往九

ensure the accurate assessment of customs duties to be paid on imports and exports, but over time it became involved in many activities including the erection of lighthouses and navigation aids along China's coast and waterways, the survey of coasts and rivers, the collection of local waterway dues such as bund, bridge, river and wharfage, weather reporting, the interruption of smuggling and the prevention of disease from ship-borne infection. It also created trade statistics and trade reports and hundreds of monographs dealing with items of merchandise from silks and furs to ginseng, tea and opium. It helped China participate in almost thirty international exhibitions, acted as informal intermediary between China and foreign representatives and guided China in training her first diplomats, thus laying the foundation for the Consular and Diplomatic Services. The last duty undertaken by the Customs Service was the administration of the postal service, which it ran until 1911 when it was financially strong enough to be subsumed into the Board of Posts and Communications.

It is no wonder that my father found his life interesting!

After the fall of Nanjing to the Japanese in December 1937, one of the most horrendous episodes ever known in wartime, my father was ordered to sail to Jiujiang and he informed my mother that he would return in ten days. In fact, it was thirteen months before he would see her again. In Shanghai, the British Consul announced that British subjects should depart for Hong Kong. So many of my mother's friends were leaving and urged her to go, but with my father up-river and unreachable it was a difficult decision to make on her own. She finally decided she should leave Shanghai and had all the household goods shipped later by the houseboy who carefully packed up everything to the last teaspoon.

On arrival in Hong Kong she went to a recommended guest house on Mody Road, Kowloon, and felt comfortable in the British way of life of the territory. Hong Kong had the busiest harbour in the world, and like Shanghai it was exotic and exciting. But my mother had left a job in banking to go out to Shanghai, and now finding herself on her own in Hong Kong she did not want to sit and do nothing. She heard there was a job vacancy in a shop named The Caravan, which was on the ground floor of the prestigious Peninsula Hotel, and she quickly applied. The shop sold Chinese brocades, fine china, Chinese jewellery and pure-silk ladies underwear. The owner, Eileen Kershaw (who later became my godmother), re-established the shop after the Second World War in 1947 under her own name. Both she and her husband were interned in Stanley Camp where sadly he died. The shop was to continue under several different owners after she retired to the United Kingdom.

My father had finally joined my mother in Hong Kong from Shanghai in early 1939 and they lived in an attractive house with a large verandah on Prat Avenue but no one then thought that Hong Kong would ever fall. In Hong Kong, my mother had continued to work at The Caravan, and she played tennis and hockey at the weekends. She played hockey for Hong Kong in the Interport against Shanghai, having previously played for Shanghai against Hong Kong in 1937.

She had little interest or time for the more leisurely pursuits of mahjong, tea parties, and bingo, with which other women kept themselves occupied. However, by mid-

江，他告訴母親十日後回來，結果十三個月後他倆才得以重聚。那時上海的英國領事宣佈，所有英國人應出發前往香港，母親的許多朋友都敦促她一同離開。由於父親正在途上無法聯絡，孤身的母親徬徨難於抉擇。她最終選擇離開上海，所有的家當以至一根茶匙，都由男僕小心包裝後運到香港。

甫抵達香港，她即住進一所人家推介，位於九龍麼地道的賓館，這裡的英式生活令她頓覺舒暢。香港擁有世界上最繁忙的港口，也像上海一樣，有令人感到興奮的異國風情。離開上海，她失去了銀行的工作，卻不願終日坐著無所事事。當她聽到尊貴的半島酒店地下有一家叫「加拿芬」的店鋪招人，即趕快應徵；店鋪專門售賣來自中國的織錦，中式珠寶及女士真絲內衣。二戰後的一九四七年，東主顧愛蓮女士（即後來我的教母），以自己的名字作店名重新開業，她們夫婦倆都曾被關進赤柱集中營，丈夫更不幸死於營中。她退休後返回英國，店鋪之後多次易手，但仍繼續經營。

一九三九年初，父親終於從上海到港和母親重聚，他們住在寶勒巷一棟擁有大陽台的誘人房子；誰也沒想到香港也將淪陷。在香港，母親繼續於「加拿芬」工作，週末則以網球及曲棍球作消遣。她代表香港在曲棍球埠際賽中與上海對壘。而一九三七年的時候，她則代表上海出戰香港。

正當其他婦女忙於麻雀耍樂，喝下午茶及玩Bingo遊戲，母親對這些卻興趣索然。一九四零年中，歐洲戰事不斷惡化，日軍正朝著香港邊境進發，本地的生活正面臨嚴重轉變。雖然很多人不願相信戰爭會在香港爆發，但一九四零年六月某天，父親致電母親，指示她拿一件小行李和個人財物，準備乘船前往澳洲。

第一次海上旅程

當時的我才七個月大，我是在一九三九年十一月十六日晚上八時，兔年的一個晚上在九龍醫院出生。出生的時候，父親正值海上，街上沒有的士，母親只有招了一輛人力車前往亞皆老街的產房，車伕瞥了母親一眼即全速直奔，他大概不想充當一位為鬼婆分娩的助產士。一個月後，我在彌敦道的聖安德烈教堂受洗。俚語「鬼婆」是指一位有歐洲血統的外籍婦人，可能是由於膚色的原因，一種帶有貶意的稱呼，廣東話的意思是「女鬼」。但幾十年下來，已演變成口頭上對居於香港的白種女人的稱謂。

九龍醫院始建於一九二二年，在一個叫大石鼓的山崗上興建，一九二五年落成。一幢擁有三十四張病牀的產科大樓於一九三二年落成，以應付九龍區人口迅速膨漲，這幢今天的M座大樓，擁有兩個分科病房，基於保育原因，被評為二級歷史建築。

幸好母親聽從父親的意見，在接到他的電話兩日後和我撤退到澳洲，差不多十八個月後，一九四一年聖誕節，日本攻陷這片英國殖民地。當時的殖民地政府明白她已無力保衛香港，於是宣布所有婦孺須馬上撤離，這是倫敦下達的指示，不僅為了家眷的安全，也考慮到戰爭爆發後物資逐漸短缺，不足以養活這麼多人。由於時間緊逼來不及準備行程，大部份人都只容許 帶一件小行李，留下來的家當及個人財物，都成為搶掠者的囊中物。這是紛亂的離開，船首先航行到菲律賓，我們被安排住進一個叫麥堅利堡壘的美軍基地。直到數星期後，一艘中立船隻把我們全部人送到澳洲。

一九三八年，隨著日軍進侵華南，大量中國難民湧入香港，居住環境惡劣。預計戰爭令糧食短缺，

1940, the war in Europe was worsening and life in Hong Kong had taken on a more serious turn as it became clear that the Japanese were advancing on its border. Although many people still refused to believe that there would be war in Hong Kong, my father phoned my mother one day in late June 1940, instructing her to pack a small suitcase of belongings ready to board a ship for Australia.

First sea voyage

I was by then seven months old. I had been born at 8 p.m. in Kowloon Hospital on 16th November 1939, the Year of the Rabbit. My father was away at sea at the time and there being no taxis available, my mother had to take a rickshaw to the maternity unit on Argyle Street. The rickshaw coolie took one look at my mother and took off at top speed – he was not about to become a midwife to a *gweipo*. I was christened at St. Andrew's Church, Nathan Road a month later. The slang term "gweipo", meaning a foreign woman of European descent (literally a "ghost woman" in Cantonese, because of the fair skin), had at the time a derogatory edge, but over the decades it has passed into the colloquial terminology of Caucasian residents of Hong Kong.

Construction of Kowloon Hospital had begun in 1922 on a hill known as Tai Shek Ku and was completed in 1925. The maternity block was added later and completed in 1932 with thirty-four beds to cope with the rapid increase of the Kowloon population. Now known as Block M, it is still there today and is a Grade 2 listed building with two authentic wards that are preserved for heritage reasons.

Fortunately, my mother heeded my father's advice and two days following his call, she and I were evacuated to Australia, although it was to be almost eighteen months before the Japanese captured the British Crown Colony on Christmas Day 1941. The colonial government at the time knew that there was no way of defending Hong Kong against the Japanese and announced that all women and children must leave immediately. This was a directive from London, not only from regard to the safety of dependants but because should war break out it would mean there would be fewer mouths to feed on dwindling supplies. There was very little time to prepare for the sea voyage and most passengers were only allowed to carry one small suitcase. Household effects and personal items all had to be left behind and the looters soon seized their chance. It was a chaotic departure, and we sailed first to the Philippines where we were accommodated at Fort McKinley, an American army base, for several weeks until a neutral ship could be made available to take us all on to Australia.

Following the extension of Japanese operations in southern China in 1938 there had been a huge influx of Chinese refugees into Hong Kong and most of these were still living in appalling conditions. Anticipating the food shortages of war, many chose to return to their native villages in China, but many others remained to see out the war years in Hong Kong. During the occupation, Chinese civilian officials ran an administrative system in the territory to keep things running, dourly accepting Japanese military supervision.

We had sailed to Manila with over two thousand other Europeans on the newly fitted troopship ironically named *Empress of Japan*. My mother must have had her heart in her mouth as she said goodbye to my father, not knowing when or if they would ever meet again.

部份難民選擇回鄉，留下來的見證了香港的淪陷歲月。日本佔領期間，中國籍文職人員在日軍的嚴苛監管下，繼續維持這地方的行政系統如常運作。

我們和其他二千多名歐洲人，乘坐一艘戰艦先到馬尼拉，諷刺的是這艘軍艦叫「日本皇后號」。母親與父親道別的時候，實則已是膽顫心驚，因不知何日或還有機會見面否。

我們被安排入住船艙的共用大房間，育嬰設施不足，我被逼要與母親同牀。用餐的食堂已算是宏偉，但仍不足以容納所有人同時進食，故需輪流用餐，母親用餐時，需把我交托友人照顧，其他的母親如是。母親們都得排隊在洗臉盆清洗尿布等，而在船艙晾乾需時很長。

正值季侯風季節，經過三十六小時的顛簸旅程，船上各人大多感到不適及暈浪。船在大雨中靠岸，乘客由軍車送往麥堅利堡壘。我們被安排入住一所兩層高的木製建築物。建築物底部用木樁加高，防止大雨時受到水淹。營房的床，寢具及蚊帳等都是簇新的。每人獲分派一隻碟，刀具及錫杯，食物看來相當充裕。

在那裡每天無所事事，有關香港的消息亦欠奉。數天後，兩艘船送來了從香港來的逃難者，先來的需遷往別處，以騰出地方給新來的人。他們被送到馬尼拉的不同地方，住處大多能接受和受歡迎。但其中一群被安置於歷史古城"因特拉穆羅斯"的，則懇求紅十字會讓他們遷到別的地方，因那裡的床滿佈木虱，老鼠和蟑螂亦到處出沒，紅十字會的人雖很體貼的為他們找尋新居所，但由於投訴的人眾多，工作艱巨，況且他們都是過客，何時離開及去向皆未能確定。

僅有的消息顯示，所有的逃難者都會被送往澳洲。不知何故，一群自許較有認識的卻選擇返回香港，要知道那些最初容許留在香港的婦女，都是一些必需服務及醫療服務的志願工作者。現在這群回歸的人，卻欠缺那些技能。正如政府預測，她/他們回去後都被關進赤柱監獄，亦間接攤薄了那些留下來作戰的男人的糧食。

度過了在菲律賓的漫長六星期，第一批的逃難者終於乘坐一艘荷蘭輪船前往澳洲，我們最終也踏上旅途。

抵達澳洲

一九四零年十月，我們抵達悉尼，下船後被送往一家酒店住了一個晚上。第二天早上，我們乘火車前往阿德雷德，我的祖父母就住在那裡。待在那裡一個月，母親收不到任何戰爭的消息。剛好她其中一個兄弟，正是在皇家海軍服役的海軍中尉，乘船抵達悉尼，母親於是前往悉尼會他，他告知香港很快便會落入日軍手中。母親之後返回阿德雷德，但她認為只有長期留在悉尼，才可以獲得大量有關遠東及太平洋戰爭的消息；得到祖父母的允許，母親和我移居悉尼。

但這樣母親的積蓄很快便會花光，須找份工作以維持生計。一天，母親在邦迪海灘坐著的時候，碰上一位丈夫在「標準真空油公司」當主管的女士，她說可讓丈夫為母親謀個職位。言出必行，兩天後，母親果真在上午接受面試，下午便受僱。無比的好運之餘還是存有暗湧，周歲嬰兒不可能獨留家中，總得找個托居的地方。

一位住在屈臣氏灣叫波爾太太的女士，帶着兩個女兒和兩個中國女傭從上海走出來，她收容那些母親需外出工作的小孩。這不是一個理想的選擇，

We were accommodated in a dormitory on board in the public rooms but very little provision had been made for babies who had to share their mother's camp bed. Meals were held in the magnificent dining rooms but they were not large enough to hold everyone at once, so several sittings were needed. While my mother ate, she would hand me over to a friend to be looked after, as did other mothers with babies. The mothers also had to queue at washbowls to wash out nappies etc., which took a very long time to dry below decks.

After thirty-six hours of a rather rough and uncomfortable voyage (it being the monsoon season) when nearly everyone on board was seasick, the ship docked in the pouring rain and the passengers were loaded onto army trucks and taken to Fort McKinley. They were found accommodation in wooden two-storied buildings which were on stilts to avoid flooding in heavy rains – such as there were at that time – with camp beds, bedding and mosquito nets that were all new. Each person was given a plate, some cutlery, and a tin mug. It seems food was plentiful.

There was nothing to do each day and no news of Hong Kong reached them, but after a few days, two more ship loads of evacuees arrived from Hong Kong and the first arrivals had to be moved to make room for the newcomers. They were taken to different locations in Manila, where mostly the accommodation was acceptable and welcome. However, one group that had been housed in the historic walled city of Intramuros pleaded with the Red Cross to move them elsewhere because the hotel's beds were bug infested and the place was alive with cockroaches and rats. The Red Cross was very obliging in finding better quarters but its job was tough with so many people complaining, particularly that they had no confirmation as to when or to where they would be moved on.

What little news filtered in suggested that all the evacuees would definitely be sent to Australia. There were many, however, who thought they knew better and somehow managed to return to Hong Kong. The only women who had been initially allowed to stay in Hong Kong were those in the essential services and nursing volunteers. Those who returned had none of these skills and were unpopular when they were interned in Stanley Prison because, as Whitehall had predicted, it meant less food for the men who had stayed behind to fight.

Finally, after a long six weeks in the Philippines, the first load of evacuees was put on a Dutch ship for Australia. We were on our way at last.

Arrival in Australia
We arrived in Sydney in October 1940 and after disembarkation we were taken to a hotel for the night. The next morning we caught a train to Adelaide where my paternal grandparents were then living. We stayed there for a month but my mother began to realise that she was getting no news of the war. One of her brothers, who was a lieutenant commander in the Royal Navy, arrived in Sydney on his ship and my mother travelled to Sydney to meet him. He told her that Hong Kong would soon fall to the Japanese. She returned to Adelaide but realising that she would get a great deal more news of the war in the Far East and Pacific if she were permanently in Sydney, we moved there with my grandparents' permission and approval.

在別無他選的情況下，我還是要寄居她家裡。往後數年，我只有在每周六午飯後，母親下班才能見到她；星期日黃昏，頓足尖叫的我又被拖回屈臣氏灣。這數年間，母親憂戚與共，就是擔心幾近音訊全無的父親，除了首年收到兩張經日本人審查過，寫有寥寥二十五字的明信片外，往後音訊杳然。

我討厭每個周日回去，不喜歡那中國女傭把我獨個兒留在漆黑的廚房裡，皆因我不肯進食她們為我準備的熱牛奶泡粟米片。直到今天，想起那泡軟了的熱牛奶粟米片仍想嘔吐。由於當地沒有幼兒院，我每日的工作，就是看著鄰居森姆叔叔料理園藝，他在第一次世界大戰中失去雙腿；或許是從小便接觸，我一直鍾愛植物。

一天當我們在花園的時候，有幾個美國水手帶著玩具來訪，他們讓小孩們挑喜歡的玩具，我挑了一只羊毛造的可愛的「考拉熊」，自此它從沒有離開我的視線範圍。它是我人生的第一只玩具，玩具在戰時十分稀有，一直伴我多年，但傷心的是飛蛾吃掉它大部份的羊毛，我不得已把它扔掉。

除了擔心杳無音訊的父親，母親還需工作以維持生計，慶幸波爾太太能收留我，母子倆總算是自由和安全。

囚在赤柱的父親

我父親可沒那麼幸運，一九四一年聖誕日，這片英國殖民地落入日本人手中。他和其他在港的歐洲人一起被關進赤柱監獄。在那裡，他們立即投入清理日軍轟炸所造成的破壞，父親隨後被安排到清潔衛生隊。一九四二年一月起，監獄連同聖士提反書院也變為集中營，關押着大約二千八百名男，女和小孩。隨着越來越多被關押的人患上痢疾或腸道疾病，再加上水源配給，要將廁所排空及清潔乾淨實在是一件非常艱巨的任務。隨後父親被安排掘墳殯葬死難者，由於資源匱乏，他甚至要將破底的衣櫃改裝成棺木，除兩人以外，其他死者的棺木都要循環再用。

持續的糧食短缺，令人們終日生活在惶恐飢餓當中，就算幸運地能嘗到米飯，也大多是夾雜着泥污，或從地上掃回來的。每人每星期只獲配給一安士半的肉及八安士的米飯。

集中營的生活極為艱苦，營友來自社會不同階層，彼此相處並不融洽。不用說他們來自五湖四海（雖說大部份為英國人），也擁有不同的職業，教育背景和信仰，如今都被關進這個禁閉營。

據戰爭法庭在戰後所披露的證據顯示，原來有過千包由私人或紅十字會捐贈的糧食，被日軍屯積起來後運回日本。剩下在貨倉的都是那些易腐爛的食物，如巧克力，芝士等，已腐壞和長有綠色霉菌，大部份罐頭都已銹得不能觸摸。

回歸

隨著美國在廣島和長崎投下原子彈，一九四五年八月十六日，日本無條件投降，八月三十日，夏慤上將乘軍艦到港。

費沙爾上將的旗艦「約克公爵號」剛完成東京灣之旅到港，日本人就在這艦上簽署戰敗投降書，我舅父當時也在艦上。他到港後，和夏慤上將一同駕車到赤柱集中營，出席一個有二千名囚禁者參與的升旗儀式，場面令人感動。儀式完畢後，舅父的首要任務就是要找回父親，他沒有察覺原來在戰爭結束前不久，父親已被轉送到九龍馬頭涌的集中營，準備送到廣東和其他重要人士一起處決，舅父很快

However, this meant that my mother would soon run out of money for us to live on, and that she had to find a job. Sitting on Bondi Beach one day, she got talking to a woman whose husband was head of the Standard Vacuum Oil Company, and who offered to ask her husband if he could find a vacancy for her. True to her word she did just that and two days later, my mother was interviewed in the morning and employed in the afternoon. It was an enormous stroke of luck but there was a slight problem. I was only one year old and could not be left in the house alone; accommodation had to be found for me.

A lady called Mrs. Ball, who lived in Watsons Bay after leaving Shanghai with her two daughters and two amahs, was taking in children whose mothers had to work. It was not an ideal situation but the only option under the circumstances and there I went. For the next couple of years, I was to see my mother only from Saturday lunchtime, when she finished work, to Sunday evening when I would be dragged back to Watsons Bay kicking and screaming. It must have been a very difficult and emotional time for my mother who was constantly worrying about my father of whom she had had almost no news. The first year she had received two postcards with twenty-five words which had been censored by the Japanese; after that… nothing.

I hated going back each Sunday and I disliked the Chinese amahs who would leave me on my own in the kitchen in the dark because I would not eat my supper of cornflakes soaked in hot milk. Even today, I gag at the thought of it – hot soggy cornflakes! Because there were no kindergartens there was nothing to do, so I used to spend my time next door watching "Sam" gardening. Sam had lost both his legs in the

First World War, and perhaps this is where, at a very early age, I got my love of plants.

One day when we were in the garden, some American sailors came by with toys and told us children to pick any one we liked. I chose a cuddly koala bear made of lamb's wool and I never let it out of my sight. It was the first toy I had ever been given – toys being wartime scarcities – and I had it for many, many years, and I was most upset when moths ate most of the wool and it was thrown away.

But in spite of my mother's worries about not hearing from my father, having to lodge me with Mrs. Ball and trying to make ends meet, at least she and I were free and we were safe.

My father is incarcerated in Stanley

My father, however, was not so lucky. After the British Crown Colony fell to the Japanese on Christmas Day 1941, he was rounded up together with other Europeans who remained in Hong Kong and taken over to Stanley Prison where they were immediately put to work, clearing the damage caused by Japanese shelling and bombing. Together with St. Stephen's College, the prison was to become the Stanley Internment Camp and from January 1942 it housed about 2,800 men, women, and children. My father was put in the sanitary disposal team. With water rationing, it was a difficult task to keep the toilets emptied and clean, particularly when more and more internees suffered from dysentery and other intestinal problems. This was followed by a stint as a grave digger and since there were no coffins, he found an old wardrobe with a false bottom that was used and re-used for all funerals except two.

就得悉此事並找到父親。就在日本人於半島酒店簽署投降書的當天，舅父邀請父親到「約克公爵號」艦上共晉午餐，面對久違了三年半的美食，尤其是啤酒，父親還是能保持一點矜持。

父親被釋放的時候體重只剩得6石(84磅)，對於身高接近六呎的人來說是過輕。他接受了一次徹底的健康檢查，除了膽石劇痛，養養不良及視力欠佳之外，健康尚算正常。

沒多久，父親便可以乘坐皇家軍艦「溫德斯號」到澳洲，當時五歲的我，從沒見過父親一面。母親和我一早便到悉尼的碼頭等候，迎接父親。那一刻，害羞蓋過了我的興奮心情，在此之前數月，我才知道有父親的存在。

父親抵達悉尼後，我們舉家再次前往阿德雷德探望年邁的祖父母，這次也是他們最後一次見面。經過數月的休息和享用美食，一九四五年聖誕，我們登上往悉尼的火車，準備另一次史詩式的旅程。每年這段時間，乾熱的風無情地吹，悉尼氣溫高達45°C。我們這次是前往英國，七星期後，抵達南安普頓。說實話，這不是一個愉快的旅程，我們乘坐的是一艘滿載聯軍戰俘回國的運兵船，艦上老鼠到處出沒。基於某些原因，艦上指揮官也不滿軍艦用來接載平民，可能是他沒有管束平民的權力，也因此令軍隊之間產生不滿。從南安普頓，我們再前往什羅普，住在我的另一位舅父家中，他是埃爾斯米爾一家銀行的經理。

回到香港
四個月後，父親從膽石手術中康復，健康漸入佳境。中國海事海關重召父親回中國繼續工作，畢竟住宿地方仍然緊張，基於安全考慮，婦孺並不適合前往，母親和我於是繼續住在什羅普。

一九四七年，我們回到香港，父親繼續他在中國海事海關的工作，但運氣老是跟他對着幹。抗日戰爭結束，國共血腥內戰重啓，經過長達二十二年的戰鬥，共產黨取得勝利，蔣介石敗走寶島(台灣)。外國人為中國海事海關服務劃上句號，父親也跟著掉職。

一九四七年乘船回港的旅程，至今仍歷歷在目，尤其是那些跑到船上來，玩魔術娛樂我們的埃及塞德港的傳奇魔術師；以及跳進海中撿拾我們掉進去硬幣的當地小孩。我第一次泳池游泳的經驗卻惹怒母親，她每晚進食晚餐前會讓我先上牀睡覺，而我卻有更佳的去處－就是到泳池游泳，泳池水深八呎沒有淺水端，我抓着欄杆拉動自己圍着泳池泅，直至我聽到母親怒吼：「給我馬上離開泳池」！就像蜜蜂碰到蜜糖，多大的驚嚇也無法阻止我游下去。一天我已能撥水從一角游到另一角，我的自豪換來屁股受難。母親可能也不知道這只是我游泳生涯的開始；後來我在說英語的九龍梳士巴利道青年會，接受了一段時間的游泳訓練。

六星期後，我們抵達香港的九龍倉，父親已在碼頭接船。這是我第一次坐上人力車，我坐在母親膝上，父親則乘另一輛。七年後重回我的出生地 － 九龍，興奮莫名！

我在尖沙咀的童年
我的童年生活大都在尖沙嘴度過，今天的遊客，初來步到的人和年輕一代已很難想像昔日的境況。不僅是那時候很多的建築物，大多已失去踪影；令人傷感的是，有更多的中國傳統文化，都隨着時間流

Food was an ongoing problem and constantly on the internees' minds as they felt such appalling hunger. If they were lucky to be given rice, it was usually full of dirt and gravel, and sometimes floor sweepings. Rations consisted of one-and-a-half ounces of meat a week with eight ounces of rice.

Life in Stanley Camp was very harsh and not always conducted in an atmosphere of co-operation as the internees were from many different walks of life, persuasions and educational backgrounds, not to mention nationalities (although most were British), and were now thrown together at close quarters.

After the war, evidence emerged at the war trials that thousands of private and Red Cross food parcels were stockpiled by the Japanese with a great deal going to Japan. Parcels which had been stored in the godowns and contained items such as chocolate, cheese, and other perishables were rotten and green with mildew. Most canned goods were rusty and untouchable.

Repatriation

Following the dropping of the bombs on Hiroshima and Nagasaki and the Japanese surrender on 16th August 1945, Admiral Harcourt sailed into Hong Kong waters on 30th August.

My uncle (my mother's brother) was on HMS *Duke of York*, which was Admiral Fraser's flagship and had just completed her voyage from Tokyo Bay, Japan, where the Japanese surrender was signed. He drove with Admiral Harcourt to Stanley for an emotional flag raising ceremony attended by 2,000 internees.

The first thing my uncle did was to look for my father, but he was not aware that just before the war ended, he had been moved to another camp, Ma Tau Chung in Kowloon, to await transport to Guangzhou to be executed together with other key men. However, having very quickly found this out, my uncle invited my father for lunch on board the *Duke of York* on the day the surrender was signed in Hong Kong in the Peninsula Hotel. My father had not seen food like this for three-and-a-half years and had to be very restrained, especially with the beer.

On release from Stanley, my father weighed six stone (eighty-four pounds) – not much for a man of nearly six feet. He was given a thorough medical check-up and apart from very painful gall stones, malnutrition, and poor eyesight, he was declared reasonably fit.

Not long after this, my father was able to get a passage to Australia on HMS *Vindex*. I was five years old and had never seen him. My mother and I were on the wharf in Sydney to meet him and I was very excited till the moment came and shyness overtook me. It took several months before I understood that I now had a father as well.

Following his arrival in Sydney, we travelled once more to Adelaide so that my father could see his elderly parents, whom he was never to see again. After a couple of months of good food and rest there, we boarded a train for Sydney on Christmas Day 1945, where we were to take a ship on yet another epic journey. The temperature in Sydney was 45°C and the hot dry wind, so common at that time of the year, blew relentlessly. This time we were heading for Britain and arrived in Southampton about seven weeks later. It was not a pleasant journey because we were travelling on a troopship

逝而蕩然無存。七十年後的今天，看着到處高樓大廈林立，很難相信一九四七年的時候，我們竟無容身之所；翻看舊照片答案很快揭曉－它們大都受到破壞。戰後初期香港島最高的建築物是舊匯豐銀行總行，九龍則是半島酒店(還沒有新建的後座新翼)。香港島矗立着很多宏偉的歷史建築如：最高法院大樓，座落在畢打街街角的舊郵政總局和它對面的於仁行，還有維港岸邊的英皇大廈；但不旋踵它們都讓路予今天的玻璃幕牆大廈。

戰爭結束，轟炸，炮擊及搶掠造成廣泛破壞，香港的住屋仍極為匱乏，政府於是要求半島酒店騰出兩層的房間，給予所需工種的回流工人，包括我父親在內的獲釋戰俘，公務員，以及因戰爭失去家園的香港居民暫住。事實很快證明，兩個樓層的房間根本不足以應付殖民地的住屋需求。再加上要提供住宿給那些協助香港重建的工人，還要收容數以百計不同國籍無家可歸的人，環境實在十分擁擠。宴會廳也有一段時間被改裝成四十個睡房，我們幸運地獲分配一個房間，酒店也曾因為同一時間容納二千人居住而聞名。

舉世知名的半島酒店於一九二八年十二月開業，被推廣為蘇彝士運河以東最佳酒店，很快便成為城中最主要的社交地方，一九三零年代已接待不少荷里活明星。日治時期，它被日軍徵用為行政中心和軍事總部，外牆更被髹上迷彩色，風光不再。一九四六年末它物歸原主，地牢卻因為被炸而積水達兩呎深，變成孕育無數蚊子的理想地方。雖然如此，沒多久它再以香港社交場合的角色再現，一九四六年聖誕節，也就是日軍投降後一年，半島酒店傲然宣佈舉辦不同的慶祝活動。

儘管重修酒店的工程持續，但老鼠仍到處皆是，更不時闖入我們的房間。有一個晚上，父親出海了，我醒來乍見母親呆站房中心的椅上不敢入睡，原來有一只老鼠在房間亂竄。

開始的時候房間風扇也欠奉，更遑論冷氣機，但對於七歲的我來說，這都是無關重要的了。走廊的地氈全給日軍掠走，水泥地面正好成為我的滾軸蹓冰場。每天八元的房租維持了數年，之後調升至十元，即惹來不少投訴，皆因在當時來說，十港元已是一個不少的數目。誰會想到多年後的今天，一個酒店最好的房間，租金竟高達港幣十二萬八千元(USD16,000.-)。大概到了一九五零年代初，半島酒店回復舊觀，貴客盈門，重拾昔日光輝。

母親對半島酒店一點也不陌生，畢竟她戰前曾經在「加拿芬」工作了一段時間，但現在的情況已大不相同。在戰後物資短缺的情況下，我們一家三口很高興獲分配到一個被視為「豪華」的套間。他們當然沒想到，要在一個房間放下三張睡牀是怎樣的局促，有時也感覺非常悶熱。父親海關的工作需出海執勤，一去便數星期，母親也重新受僱於顧愛蓮女士，我因此大多時候都能獨佔房間。

最初的時候，我們三餐都在酒店進食，但新鮮感很快便消失。母親的朋友靜靜的告訴她買來一個電熱爐，並不時利用浴室作廚房，煮一些酒店不提供的菜餚。雖知此舉有違酒店規矩，母親卻覺得這是個好主意並決定仿效，只是在選購食材及菜式上要較為謹慎。然而在戰後，新鮮食材的供應仍頗為短缺，所以母親也只能弄一些相對簡單的菜式。

某年的十二月，大概是聖誕期間，有一天母親興奮的回到酒店。她不知從那裡弄來一罐罐頭聖誕布丁，打算給我們一個驚喜。母親把罐頭布丁帶到浴室，放進加了水的平底鍋裡，放在電熱板上將它

which was also a RAPWI (Repatriation of Allied Prisoners of War and Internees) vessel and was infested with rats. For some reasons also, the commanding officer resented having to carry civilians on board (possibly because he had no discipline over them) and this also encouraged a grudge among the troops. From Southampton we travelled to Shropshire and stayed with another of my mother's brothers, a bank manager in Ellesmere.

A return to Hong Kong

Four months later, having recovered from gallbladder surgery and regained better health, my father was recalled to China to continue his work with the Chinese Maritime Customs Service but it was deemed unsafe for women and children to go, and accommodation was anyway scarce, so my mother and I stayed on in Shropshire for the rest of the year.

In 1947, we returned to Hong Kong so that my father could continue his work with the Chinese Maritime Customs Service but it seemed that luck was against him again. As soon as the Japanese War was over, the Nationalists and Communists in China resumed their bloody battle, and in 1949, after twenty-two years of fighting, the Kuomintang was defeated by the Communists and Chiang Kai-shek fled to Formosa (Taiwan). This put a stop to any foreigners working for the Chinese Maritime Customs and my father then found himself without a job.

I have very vivid memories of my voyage to Hong Kong in 1947, not least of the legendary gully gully men at Port Said in Egypt who came on board to entertain with their conjuring tricks, and the local children who would climb up the ship and dive for coins we threw into the sea. It was also my first experience of a swimming pool, which caused my mother much anguish. She would put me to bed each night while she went to dinner, but I had better things to do and the swimming pool called. In a pool with a depth of eight feet and no shallow end, I would cling to the rail and pull myself round and round until I heard an angry voice say, "Get out of there at once!" No amount of threats could keep me from doing this: it was like honey to a bee. One day I just let go and paddled from corner to corner but all I got for my pride was a smacked bottom! Little did my mother know that this was just the start of a swimming career, of lessons and hours of training at the pool of the English-speaking YMCA in Salisbury Road, Kowloon.

We arrived at Kowloon Wharf, Hong Kong, six weeks later where my father met us at the dockside. Here I had my first ride in a rickshaw; I sat on my mother's lap in one and my father took off in another. I was back in Kowloon where I had been born just over seven years earlier, and excitement lay at my feet!

My childhood in Tsim Sha Tsui

It would be difficult for visitors, newcomers, and the younger generation today to visualise the Hong Kong of my childhood, which was mostly spent in Tsim Sha Tsui. Not only have many of the buildings constructed at that period disappeared, but sadly, so too have many Chinese cultural traditions. Looking at the tall crowded buildings seventy years later, I can hardly believe that there was no accommodation available for us in 1947, but old photos soon tell us why. Much of it was destroyed. The tallest building on Hong Kong Island was the old Hongkong Bank

加熱。正當我們坐在那既是睡房又是客廳的房間等著，突然聽見砰聲一響，把我們嚇得霍然站起。母親立刻推開浴室門，乍見布丁像噴泉般濺到天花板去。此時母親才意識到，應該在罐頭蓋上戳穿一個小孔，可惜這一切都為時已晚，罐頭布丁已爆濺四周，好一個聖誕驚喜！

我和朋友們對酒店內的每個角落都瞭如指掌，由住在頂層的職員，乃至住在地牢，負責每日維修和翻新工作的木匠和工人都很稔熟。另一處我們經常打擾的是閣樓的烤麵包店，那裏的廚師想藉着送上巧克力來打發我們，這反而鼓勵我們不時到訪，只因戰時我們從沒見過巧克力，那有這般享受。

酒店的兩端各有兩座升降機，操作升降機的是穿著白色制服和噊帽的機靈男童。升降機有兩道閘門，要手動把它們拉合才能令升降機運作起來。其中一名是我們這班小孩不友善地喚他「肥蘇」的操作員，他通常會在升降機沒有人的時候，讓我們來駕駛升降機。我用駕駛二字，只因讓升降機上落和水平停在要到的樓層，是要技巧地轉動一個把手來控制。很多時候我們不是停得太早就是過了頭，「肥蘇」這時便會生氣地把我們在下個樓層趕出去，但也真是樂趣無窮！如果升降機一口氣直升到六樓，我們很多時候便會急忙地上下樓層奔跑跟它競賽。

半島(我們對它的暱稱)大門外的草坪建有一座圓形多層噴水池，在熱天的時候，流水淙淙的涼快感覺實在令人難以抗拒；一天我和朋友終於按捺不住，赤腳跳進池中玩個痛快，很快我們便被父母和管家斯米諾夫太太拉出來，這個惡作劇換來的就是給她們教訓了一頓。

橫過酒店馬路，梳士巴利道和漢口道的街角交匯處，就是基督教青年會舊翼，這裡是我和朋友們課餘流連最多的地方，游泳(在一位丹麥奧運游泳選手的指導下)，打籃球和乒乓球，還有便是踩着滾軸蹓冰鞋環繞酒店，梳士巴利道，彌敦道，中間道和漢口道往返來回。

經過青年會朝天星碼頭的方向走，在梳士巴利道及阿士厘道的交_處便是消防局，小孩們覺得特別吸引。阿士厘道依舊那裡，交_點已不復存在，現建有行人隧道。雖然這地方現在已是成為一所懷舊商場的一部份，裏面還有一家叫"上海灘"的時裝店的分店，舊消防局和原有的消防車仍然守在那裡。那裡我曾經站在鐵絲網旁，希望能看到消防員出動，但事與願違，經常看到的只是消防隊中的一群錫克教徒蹲在地上，把頭髮放進盆中洗滌，洗畢便把長髮繞向頭頂結成一個髻，然後用一條指定的海軍藍色頭巾把頭髮包裹；令我看得着迷，畢竟之前沒見過有這麼長髮的男人。

酒店後面，漢口道和中間道的交匯處，青年會的對面，有一家叫「舒真高」的俄羅斯餐廳，所有侍應都是從中國南來說俄語的。我最享受的便是和父母在特別日子到那裡用晚餐，想起也令人興奮。我喜歡他們的羅宋湯和許多新穎的俄羅斯菜式如烤肉串，分派到我面前的肉串香味四逸，使我垂涎欲滴。這食肆在當年很受歡迎，接下來的年頭也廣受遊客好評。

和其他的小孩沒兩樣，我對酒店每天提供千遍一律的菜式－肉類，魚和兩種蔬菜，毫不感興趣，母親為我沒有把盤子裡的食物吃光感到苦惱。我不在乎那些年頭糧食短缺，又或曾經是戰俘的父親認為浪費食物是暴殄天物，無知的我，就是怎樣也提不起食慾。在半島的午膳時間，每當我的摯友和她家

and the tallest in Kowloon, the Peninsula hotel (without the recently added rooms at the back). There were some architecturally magnificent buildings on Hong Kong Island such as the Supreme Court, the Post Office on the corner of Pedder Street and the wonderful Union Building opposite, with King's Building on the waterfront. They would soon disappear to make way for the modern glass and chrome edifices of today.

When war ended, living accommodation was in such great shortage because of the widespread destruction – whether from bombing, shelling or looting – that the Hong Kong government requisitioned two floors of the Peninsula hotel for essential workers returning to Hong Kong, released prisoners of war (POWs) including my father, civil servants and Hong Kong residents who had lost their homes. But two floors soon proved to be totally inadequate for the colony's accommodation needs. In addition to billeting the essential workers engaged in trying to get Hong Kong back on its feet, the Peninsula was to serve as the headquarters for the Kowloon Military Administration and to house hundreds of Hong Kong's homeless of all nationalities in very cramped conditions, the ballroom at one stage being converted into forty bedrooms. The hotel is reputed to have sheltered as many as two thousand people at one time. We were lucky to get a room to ourselves!

The world-famous Peninsula hotel, which had opened in December 1928 and been promoted as the "finest hotel east of the Suez", had quickly become the city's foremost social meeting place and in the 1930s had welcomed several of Hollywood's stars. But during the war the hotel was used as the Japanese administrative centre and military headquarters

and was no longer in the best condition. It was returned to its owners at the end of 1946 with rainwater two feet deep in the basement, the result of structural bombing damage, making it the perfect breeding ground for millions of mosquitoes, and with its external walls painted in camouflage! However, it hadn't taken long for Hong Kong's social scene to re-emerge after the Japanese surrender the year before, and by Christmas 1946 the Peninsula was already proudly announcing various entertainments.

Despite the continuing repair work at the hotel, rats and mice abounded and made their way to our room. One night, when my father was away at sea, I woke up to see my mother standing on a chair in the middle of the floor; she'd seen a mouse run around the skirting and was afraid to go to bed!

There were no fans in the rooms to begin with and air conditioning was a far-off luxury but to me as a seven-year-old, it was of no consequence. The Japanese had looted all the corridor carpets so the concrete surface was perfect for roller skating! The rent was eight dollars per day for a room and when, after a couple of years, it was raised to ten dollars, there were a lot of complaints. Ten Hong Kong dollars was considered a large amount of money at that time but recently the best rooms in the hotel have been quoted as costing over one hundred and twenty-eight thousand Hong Kong dollars a night (USD16,000)! It was probably not until the very early 1950s that the Peninsula returned to anything like normality as a hotel and once again received its glamorous guests.

Of course, my mother had known the hotel before the war from her days working at The Caravan, but the situation now was rather different. Here we were, three of us living

人用膳完畢，就會走過來我們的飯桌，在我父母不在意的時候，用餐巾把我剩下討厭的煮馬鈴薯包起來帶走處理掉。回想起來，這真的可惡！你別管，我就是不會餓死。

我到了「京高斯」餐廳就沒有這問題了，它位於彌敦道，今天九龍清真寺的對面，老闆是和藹可親的京高斯先生。這家餐廳主打窩夫餅和香蕉熱鬆餅並配以大量糖漿，當然更少不了招牌草莓奶昔。這些都是我的至愛，在這裡我可食慾旺盛。跟父親一樣，來自美國的京高斯先生也曾是赤柱集中營的戰俘，現在看來嚴重超重的他，掙回的體重應遠比他在營中失去的多。韓戰期間，他的餐廳很受美國士兵歡迎。

朝北京道的方向走，過不了幾個店舖，便是一家叫「紅獅子」的酒吧。它的兩扇晃門就好像牛仔電影中酒吧所用的一樣。黃昏時份，父母外出，我總愛坐在窗前(房間就在面向漢口道那邊的五樓)，看着那些剛打完架的水手奪門而出，縱身跳上人力車，叱喝車伕趕快上路，互相追逐，年幼單純的我看得樂不可支。

可能目睹這些，促使我作出另一些的惡作劇。一九二八年前，藍色的士還沒在九龍出現，而勞斯萊斯車隊更遠未投入服務之前，人力車可算是當時來往尖沙嘴及周邊的主要交通工具，長久以來，半島酒店都容許它們停泊在大門口接載賓客。

當人力車停靠等客的時候，車伕們大部分時間都是睡在車旁的地上或陰涼的地方，沒有看管好這些交通工具。就是這個機會，那個和我一起跳進半島噴水池的朋友，她坐上人力車，而我就站到拉桿的中間，使力拉起她及人力車，我終於能起步及左轉入彌敦道，好不容易跑了數碼，便聽到車伕大叫「哎吔」的跑上來，從我的手上搶回拉桿，我的朋友從車上翻了出來，我倆趕緊逃命，剩下車伕獨自跑回酒店。

在北京道和漢口道的轉角處是明星戲院，我大部分的零用錢都花在這裏；戲票每張八毫，我和朋友只買一張戲票，共用一個座位而竟沒有人阻止；時至今天我還在想，我們是怎樣過關的。所有的電影都是黑白片，加利谷巴的「龍城殲霸戰」和珍羅素的「亡命之徒」(我成年之後才知道這部影片原來已被禁多年)，還有差理卓別靈，兩傻電影系列，當然更少不了「泰山」。

半島酒店對面，彌敦道的街角，即今天的喜來登酒店，從前是一片大空地，那裏是我和朋友踢足球，踏單車的地方，也是香港中華廠商聯合會每年用來舉辦展覽會的場地。但最激動人心的還是當年有馬戲團來訪，就在這地方搭建帳幕，表演期長達一個月。我們不時前往與小丑們和表演者聊天，又匐伏帳幕內看他們綵排，歡樂的時光總是苦短。糟糕！轉眼又過了回家的時間。

馬戲團來到後不久的一個早上，一覺醒來發現喉嚨十分腫脹，原來我得了腮腺炎。作為小孩，腦海第一時間想到的是不用上學，喜出望外瞬間變為失望，皆因意識到生病的我同樣不能到馬戲團去。更令我生氣的是朋友們回來說，他們跟馬戲團小丑們暢談一番，並趁著表演者排練的時候嘗試當空中飛人。

過了不久，香港天文台發出了颱風即將來臨的警告。正當我們都在猜測到底馬戲團的帳篷是否要被拆除，最終颱風轉向遠離，而帳篷幾近完好無缺，但帳幕的天花卻撕開了一大塊。此時的我已經康復

in one room with an adjoining bathroom. We were glad to have any accommodation at all, but although it might have been considered "luxurious" in the post-war situation of shortage, with three beds in the room it was very cramped and constraining, and at times very hot. However, as my father would often be away at sea on the Customs ship for a couple of weeks at a time and my mother had returned to work for Eileen Kershaw, I often had the room to myself.

Initially, we ate in the hotel, but the novelty soon wore off. A friend of my mother's quietly let it be known that she had bought an electric ring and was from time to time cooking in their bathroom to provide alternative meals. My mother thought this an excellent idea and decided to do the same. However, knowing that it wasn't something the hotel would encourage she was very circumspect in what she bought and cooked. There was very little fresh food available anyway and her meals were accordingly simple.

One December, around Christmas time, she came back to the hotel very excited. She had found a tinned Christmas pudding somewhere and had decided to give us a surprise treat by heating it up in a saucepan of boiling water on the hotplate in the bathroom. Unfortunately, she didn't realise – until it was too late – that she had omitted to puncture the lid. As we were sitting next door in the bedroom-cum-sitting room there was a sudden BANG and we all shot to our feet. My mother pushed open the bathroom door to find a fountain of Christmas pudding hitting the ceiling. The can had exploded and there was pudding everywhere. So much for our Christmas surprise!

My friends and I knew every inch of the hotel from the roof top where the staff lived, to the basement where the carpenters and workers carried out their daily maintenance and renovation. One of our favourite haunts was the bakery on the mezzanine floor; the chef would give us chocolates to get rid of us but this only encouraged us to return another day! What a treat that was, especially as we had not seen chocolate during the war years.

At each end of the hotel were two elevators each with a very smart lift boy dressed in a white uniform and cap. There were two gates to the lift which he had to pull across before it would function. If we got in the lift and there were no other passengers, "Fatso", which we children unkindly referred to one of the boys as, used to let us have a turn at driving the lift. I say driving because a handle had to be turned and it took some skill to bring the lift car up or down, level with the floor. More often than not we shot past the floor or stopped too soon; Fatso would then get angry and push us out at the next floor. It was all a lot of fun! The lift went all the way up to the sixth floor, but most of the time we were in a hurry and ran up and down trying to race it.

Outside the front entrance of "the Pen" (as it was affectionately known) was a large green manicured lawn with a round tiered fountain and trickling water. This was very tempting on a hot day. One such day a friend and I decided to have a paddle but we were soon pulled out and I got into big trouble for my escapade from both my parents and the housekeeper, Mrs. Smirnoff.

Across from the hotel on the corner of Salisbury Road and Hankow Road was the old building of the YMCA. That was where my friends and I spent most of our time after school, swimming (under the watchful eye of Lykke Rose, a Danish Olympic swimmer), playing basketball and table

了，和朋友從半島酒店向下望，可以透過破洞觀看馬戲團的表演，而且是免費的，可謂因禍得福。

你可想像我們除了上學以外，課餘時間並非每一刻都那麼充實，所以惡作劇也特別多。為了打發時間而又求方便就手，這天朋友和我便決定到酒店的頂層六樓，所說的蜜月套房樓層去探秘。在那裏，我們發現一柄梯子倚在走廊牆上，通往上面一個僅能容得下我們鑽進去的小洞。我先爬進去看個究竟，只見裏頭是一個偌大的空間，地上很多被電線蓋着的木樑，我轉身下來，她也想爬進去一看。我警告不要踏在電線上，她就踏在電線與電線之間，但瞬即失去蹤影；我急忙爬進去找她，探頭看見她已從一個大洞掉到十呎下面的一張大牀旁，大牀也被她壓垮了。我趕忙從梯子走下來，稍鬆一口氣的是她已從房間跑出來，只是腳脛已被金屬牀架劃破淌血，痛楚呻吟，我們抬頭望一下天花的大洞便一溜煙的跑掉。今天我們回想到這一幕仍相對大笑，因為如果被抓起來，後果真的不堪設想！

經過艱巨的工程和克服不少困難，九廣鐵路終於在一九一零年十月投入服務，火車早期只行走英界部分，也就是由中港邊境的羅湖至尖沙嘴的天星碼頭旁，今天尖沙嘴鐘樓矗立的地方。火車行經半島酒店前面的另一段梳士巴利道，這片土地今天建有文化中心和太空館。一九一一年，至廣州的中界部分也正式開通，而九龍也成為了始自歐洲的環西伯利亞鐵路的終點站。

寂靜的晚上，我常聽見沉重的蒸汽機拖拉聲沿着路軌此起彼落。不管怎樣，殖民政府把精彩的舊火車總站拆卸是一項極大的錯誤，也是香港歷史其中一段最令人傷感的日子，剩下的鐘樓成為香港人的僅有集體回憶。新火車總站最終選址紅磡，但這個地點對在港島工作或住在新界的人來說，總是不太方便。

學生年代

一九四七年，我開始到位於喇沙利道和界限街交界的九龍小學唸初中，那時候從尖沙嘴到九龍塘感覺就好像出國那麼遠。每天早上，我在半島酒店漢口道出口那邊等乘校巴，那是一輛工務局的舊卡車，沒幾輛巴士能完好的在戰爭中倖存下來，卡車尾端掛有鐵梯供上落，車廂兩旁有長櫈可坐。我們就把藤籃書包墊着來坐，但藤籃並不耐用。那時候並沒有我們現在的背囊或背包，我時常渴望得到一個鬆上我名字縮寫在蓋上的簇新藤籃書包。

十九世紀的時候在香港開辦一所只供英童就讀的學校，成功機會不大，主要原因是缺乏政府的支持，資金短缺和找不到合適的師資。一九零零年，得到一位非常富有和具影響力的歐亞大慈善家－何東爵士的捐助，在九龍彌敦道興建一所學校，並在一九零二年正式開辦。學校原本是希望招收不同國籍的學生（何東爵士父親是荷蘭人），只是經過一輪磋商，只接受五至十五歲的學生入讀，定名九龍英童學校。

學校歷任校長之中，對學校影響最大的，非富蘭克林南丁格爾(1916)莫屬。他高瞻遠矚，為學校成立了舊生會，籌募捐款作為學校擴張之用。正因為此，小學部得以分拆出來，並命名為九龍小學，而九龍英童學校則轉為一所中學。隨後學校不斷擴張，並在一九三六年遷至今天何文田天光道現址，新校舍被易名為中央英童學校。當時的九龍小學校舍位於覺士道，九龍木球會附近，可惜的是校舍在戰時被完全摧毀。

tennis, and roller skating round and round the hotel from Salisbury Road to Nathan Road, to Middle Road and back round Hankow Road.

Just past the YMCA going towards the Star Ferry was the fire station, a magnet for children, which was on the corner of Ashley Road and Salisbury Road. Although Ashley Road is still there, this intersection no longer exists as it is now an underground walkway, but the old fire station remains, so too an original fire truck, although it is now part of a commercial heritage complex and houses a branch of the boutique clothes shop Shanghai Tang. I used to stand by the wire fence hoping for action, but often had to settle for watching the Fire Brigade's Indian Sikhs squatting on the ground, washing their long hair in bowls. I had never seen a man with long hair before and I was fascinated, especially when I saw one tie his hair in a knot on the top of his head and then cover it with a regulation navy blue turban.

Behind the hotel on the Hankow Road side and on the corner of Middle Road opposite the YMCA was a Russian restaurant named Tkachenko's. All the waiters had come down from China and spoke Russian and my biggest treat was to go there with my parents for supper on special occasions. There was something exciting about it. I loved their borsch soup and many of the other novel Russian dishes such as shashlik. These skewered grilled cubes of meat had a delicious aromatic pungency, which was all the more mouth-watering after rationing! It was a very popular place and did well with tourists in the following years.

However, like many children, I had very little interest in eating the hotel's routine fare of meat or fish and two veg and my mother would have a dreadful time trying to get me to finish what was on my plate. It didn't matter to me that food was scarce, or that my ex-POW father saw this waste as a sacrilege; I knew no better and seemed simply to have no inclination to eat. At lunchtime at the Pen when my best friend and her parents had finished their meal, she would come and sit at our table to help me get rid of the boiled potatoes I loathed. When my parents weren't looking, she would wrap what were left in a napkin and walk out with them. Awful to think about now, but true! However, I managed to survive.

I didn't have the same problem at Gingles on Nathan Road, just opposite what is now the Kowloon Mosque. Run by the legendary, amiable Mr. Gingles, the restaurant served among other things waffles and banana hotcakes with lots of syrup, all washed down with a strawberry milkshake. That was much more to my liking! Mr. Gingles was said to be an American ex-Stanley POW, but when I knew him he was grossly oversized and had regained all the weight and more that he might have lost in camp. Gingles became very popular with US servicemen during the Korean war.

A few doors along, going towards Peking Road, was the Red Lion Pub. It had swing doors like the cowboy saloons in the movies and in the evening when my parents went out I would sit at the window (our room was on the fifth floor above Hankow Road), and watch the visiting sailors come flying out backwards through the doors after a fight. They would then get into the rickshaws and shout at the coolies to run up the road racing one another as fast as they could. As a child knowing no better, I thought this was great fun!

It was probably watching them do this that encouraged another of my childhood escapades. As rickshaws were

二戰爆發期間，中央英童學校被逼關閉，一九四六年重開。重開之時能同時收納中小學生。一九四七年學生人數急增，於是把位於喇沙利道和界限街交界的喇沙書院擴建部份接收過來，作為九龍小學的校舍，中央英童學校則變回了中學。最終在一九四八年四月三十日的學校頒獎禮上，港督葛量洪爵士宣布學校再次易名為英皇佐治五世學校，接收任何國籍的學生。

有一天我們在小學的操場中央玩波子(彈珠)的時候，發現了一件金屬物品，竟是一枚戰時日軍投下的炸彈，正當興奮的從學校撤離，軍火專家趕至準備拆除，卻發現只是一枚失效的炸彈，令我們大失所望！

一九四零年，香港政府將婦女和小孩撤離後，中央英童學校被擱置。一九四一年十二月，學校被用作軍事醫院，其後再改為治理歐洲戰俘的醫院。醫院大堂見有英國首相邱吉爾的名句「Never in the Field of Human Conflict」。醫院配備手術室和X光室，收留了大約一百三十名病人，鐘樓（現仍存在）則被用作教堂。原來的草地運動場有一部份用作種菜，另一部份則被戰俘改造成高爾夫推桿嶺和槌球場。

一九四九年，我升學到已易名為英皇佐治五世學校唸高中，直至一九五二年我離開到英國上寄宿學校。這所學校成立於一九零二年時的校舍，就在彌敦道聖安德烈教堂旁邊，這是我受洗的地方，今天的教堂已是歷史建築物。自那些年至今，我想已有數千學生及職員曾在此學習和工作。

我在學校結識了很多新朋友，有一天放學後，其中一位朋友問我可有興趣騎馬，敢於冒險的我那會錯過，兩人於是逕自走到柯士甸道槍會山軍營，那裏有小馬出租供策騎。直到今天我仍不知道當日的租馬費用何來，因為每星期一元的零用錢肯定不夠支付，那時想必是期望子債父母還。

我們騎上小馬馬背由一位士兵帶領，沿著漆咸道向九龍塘進發，那時候最遠只能走到衛理道便得轉向京士柏，往昔只是一片山頭，還沒有今天的伊利沙伯醫院或陸軍醫院。坐騎繼續前進，跨過山頭落到窩打老道，馬路中央是一條用來疏導雨水的明渠，馬路的寬度只有今天的三分之一。我們走近一條火車橋的時候，剛巧一列火車駛過，小馬受驚脫韁狂奔，我不懂把牠拉停，只知緊偎着牠保命，直至牠跑至筋疲力竭，終於在窩打老道和亞皆老街交匯處的中華電力公司外停下。

朋友的坐騎最終也趕上來，我們繼續信步前行，直至到達窩打老道盡頭，即今天的奧士本軍營。這裏有一大片紅粘土草地，引領的士兵說可讓我們在這附近慢蹓一會，可是我還沒來得及學懂控制，已被小馬毫無預警的一躍，把我摔了下來，跌進紅色泥濘的水坑。

正當我懷着興奮心情。穿著滿帶泥污的校服回到家裏，母親的怒火瞬即把我的熱情冷卻，她擔心的不僅是我從沒騎馬的經驗，最重要的是小馬在馬路上狂奔可能會令我嚴重受傷。但對於只有十歲的我來說，這次的鬧劇着實是一項創舉。後來我到英國唸寄宿學校，學會了怎樣策騎。

共產黨及它帶來的後果

一九四九年是令人難忘的一年，共產黨最終取得勝利，成千上萬的難民湧入香港。他們有徒步攀山越嶺而來，亦有乘飛機，坐船或坐火車抵達的，不管富或貧 － 都是難民。

the main form of transport in and around Tsim Sha Tsui before the advent of Blue Taxicabs (founded in Kowloon in 1928), and well before the fleet of Rolls-Royces came into being, they had long been allowed to park outside the front entrance of the Peninsula to wait for customers leaving the hotel.

Most of the time while they waited, the coolies either slept on the floor of their rickshaw or in the shade, leaving their conveyance unattended. It was on one such occasion when I and the friend with whom I had earlier paddled in the Peninsula's fountain decided to have a go. She got into the rickshaw and I stood between the shafts. Struggling to lift her and the rickshaw, I eventually took off and turned left into Nathan Road. We had hardly gone a few yards when there was a loud "Ayaaaaah!" as the coolie caught up with us and roughly grabbed the shafts from my hands. My friend tumbled out and we both ran for our lives, leaving the owner to return the conveyance to the hotel.

On the corner of Peking Road and Hankow Road was a cinema, the Star Theatre, where I spent most of my pocket money. It was eighty cents for a ticket and my friend and I would buy one ticket and share one seat. No one seemed to want to stop us but even now I wonder how we got away with it. All the movies were in black and white; Gary Cooper in *High Noon*, Jane Russell in *The Outlaw* (it was not until I was an adult that I knew that this film had been banned for many years), Charlie Chaplin, Abbott and Costello and of course, *Tarzan*.

Opposite the Peninsula hotel on the corner of Nathan Road, where the Sheraton hotel stands today, was a huge plot of open ground where we played football and rode our bikes and where the Chinese Manufacturers' Association of Hong Kong held their annual exhibition. But the biggest thrill of all was the year the circus came to town and set up on the ground for a whole month. We would go over there at any time of day and talk to the clowns and performers and crawl under the tents to watch them rehearse. Time got forgotten in that world and I often got into trouble for going home late!

The circus hadn't long arrived when I woke up one morning to find I was badly swollen around my throat: I had the mumps. The first thing that came into my mind was that I would not have to go to school. I was delighted, but this delight soon changed to disappointment when I realised that I would not be going to the circus either! I was very annoyed when my friends came back and told me they had got to talk at length with the clowns and had been able to try out the trapeze while the performers were in the tent rehearsing.

Not too long after this, the Hong Kong Observatory gave warning of an approaching typhoon and we wondered if the circus would have to be dismantled. But the typhoon veered away and the circus was left more or less intact. However, the big top now had a large rip in its roof, which allowed us the best view of all: mumps no longer a problem, my friends and I could look down into the show from the Peninsula Hotel – and it was free! "It's an ill wind etc...."

As one might imagine, there was not always a lot to keep us occupied outside school hours so we often got up to mischief. Looking for something close at hand with which to amuse ourselves one day, my friend and I decided to explore the sixth, top floor of the hotel where what were

由於住屋短缺，很多人露宿街頭，人們開始依山興建木屋來居住，導致火災頻生。隨着戰後香港復興，難民亦為香港帶來資金和勞動力，工廠和商店紛紛開辦，一些劣質的房屋也隨之而生；可是香港首個徙置區卻要等到一九五七年才在黃大仙建成，更多的徙置區亦接踵而來。無可否認的是，全靠這些本來一無所有的難民的辛勤與機智，香港才得以在戰後欣欣向榮。

一九四九年夏天，父親回家後告訴我們，他朋友即將退休回國，其位於港島都爹利街帝納大廈的住所還有三個月租期，能讓我們暫住；蘇格蘭小獵犬喬克也一併留下來。我得悉不禁喜出望外，恨不得馬上就搬進去。居半島酒店已兩年，我最大的願望卻也是無法實現的　—　就是能養一隻狗。每天放學後，我最享受的就是能和喬克到聖約翰座堂周邊玩耍，三個月的歡樂時光轉眼即逝。由於另外的住所正在興建，我們不得不回到半島酒店。

帝納大廈非常靠近座堂，當我還住在那裡時，同學們都提議我加入教堂的合唱團。心想這是一個好機會，但未知能否勝任，於是參加了合唱團每逢星期五的練習。可能是因為父母是威爾斯人，同時也是基督徒的關係，第一次練習後便被接納加入了。年青團員的練習在四時半開始，成年人會在下班後加入一起練習。在我們練習完畢等待成年人到來前的空檔時間，會趁機登上塔樓坐下來俯瞰周邊的風景。每次上去的時候門都是沒有上鎖，有一次我們被發現了，登高望遠也隨之告終。

聖誕節的時候，整個合唱團都會到不同的地方唱聖詩，如港督府(今天的禮賓府)，瑪麗醫院以及何東爵士位於山頂的大宅　—　何東花園。每次在何東花園表演完畢後，爵士都會邀請我們到大宅內舉杯暢飲，成人們一般會喝雪莉酒，而小孩則只能喝橙汁。成人們通常杯酒未盡便離開，而我卻鬼祟地把他們剩下的酒喝個清光；這一切把在旁觀看的傭人逗樂了，而我這個小合唱團成員才帶着興奮離開。

到一九五零年，我大部分朋友的父母皆為公務員，他們都獲分配入住現已重建的九龍京士柏或港島禮頓山的公務員宿舍。隨着他們離開酒店，不禁令我常常思念他們，以及一起作過的惡作劇。

我們最終也在一九五一年初遷出半島酒店，住進一幢簇新的大廈，它也是座落在一條新開闢的街道　—　金巴利街，與較長的金巴利道平行。由於街道還沒鋪上瀝青，我和朋友們便在紅土地上挖洞來練習高爾夫球推桿，加上道路上鮮有車輛走過，經常一玩便是數小時。

我和父母一起擠在酒店的一個房間近五年，不時想起能擁有自己的一個房間那份喜悅。但好景不常，翌年我被父母送到英國上寄宿學校。香港學校每班學生人數較多，父親認為一個注重思想自由與小班教學的環境下有利於我學習。離愁別緒，百般滋味在心頭！我不捨香港，因為她帶給我自由和歡樂，但我也不得不為將來作打算。

在我離港的這些年間，殖民地起了明顯變化。難民持續從中國流入，這地方也步向成為製造業樞紐，整個城市也變得興旺起來。

回來的時候，父母住在窩打老道。一九六零年，我們舉家搬進了界限街一棟兩層高的公寓，它就在明愛中心的後面，即瑪利諾修院學校斜對面；單位寬敞，有一橫跨兩邊的露台，北望獅子山的開揚景觀。我住在這裏的期間，見證了一件畢生難忘的事。我之前在香港也經歷過多次颱風，家中損毀輕

referred to as the honeymoon suites were located. We found a ladder leaning up against the corridor wall giving access into a small opening above just large enough for us to get through. I climbed up first to find out what was inside, only to see a huge empty space with wooden beams on the floor covered with electric wires. I came back down and my friend climbed up to have a look and decided to go in. I warned her not to step on the wires so she stepped between them and promptly disappeared. I climbed up again and looked through a large hole to find she had fallen at least ten feet onto the edge of a bed, which had collapsed on impact. To my relief, as I quickly retreated down the ladder she came out of the room below yelling with pain and with a bleeding leg having scraped her shin on the metal frame. We took one look at the large hole in the ceiling and ran as fast as we could. Today, we often recall the episode and still laugh about it. Had we been caught it might have been a different story!

The Kowloon–Canton Railway began its service in October 1910 after a great deal of hard work and many problems. At first, the trains were only permitted to run in the British section, i.e. from the border of China and Hong Kong at Lo Wu to the Star Ferry in Tsim Sha Tsui to where the clock tower stands today. These trains ran on the other side of Salisbury Road right in front of the Peninsula Hotel and where the Space Museum and Hong Kong Cultural Centre were eventually built. It was not until 1911 that the section to Canton finally opened, eventually making Kowloon the last stop on the trans-Siberian rail link from Europe.

Often at night I would hear the heavy steam engines shunting back and forth along the lines. The clock tower is the only reminder of that wonderful old railway terminus, the demolition of which was one of the saddest days in Hong Kong history and in my opinion, a big mistake made by the colonial government. The terminus ended up in Hung Hom, which was not considered very convenient for those working on Hong Kong Island or living in the New Territories.

School years

In 1947, I began school at Kowloon Junior School, which was situated on the corner of La Salle Road and Boundary Street, Kowloon Tong, and from our base in Tsim Sha Tsui appeared to be out in the country. Every morning, we would wait outside the Hankow Road exit of the Peninsula Hotel for the school bus, which was an old Public Works Department truck with steps attached at the back and benches to sit on inside. Few proper buses had survived the war. We carried our school books in rattan baskets and sat on them in the bus. The baskets didn't last long! There were then no such things as backpacks or rucksacks, as there are now, and I always looked forward to having a new rattan basket with my initials painted on the lid.

Attempts in the nineteenth century to open a school for British children in Hong Kong had met with limited and inconsistent success, largely because of lack of government support, shortage of funds and the difficulty of obtaining trained teachers. In 1900, Sir Robert Ho Tung, the wealthy and influential Eurasian philanthropist, came to the rescue by offering money to build a school in Kowloon, which opened in 1902 on Nathan Road. It was initially intended

微甚或沒有。但當惡名昭彰的颱風溫黛一九六二年來襲，情況卻大不一樣。

一九六二年八月二十七日，溫黛於太平洋上生成為熱帶低氣壓，距港東南偏東一千三百英哩，向西北偏西移動，並於翌日增強為強烈熱帶風暴，颱風環流直徑達一千英哩，繼續向香港方向移動。第二天黃昏，她的中心集結在香港東南偏東四百英哩，天文台掛起一號風球，風勢輕微至和緩；翌日早上，轉吹北風，風勢清勁。

八月三十一日，重光紀念日假期，三號風球懸掛。父親根據他對海洋天氣的知識，告訴我們必須帶同部份財物搬到住宅後方。當時風勢仍未算強勁，但可以肯定的是，溫黛將於翌日在非常接近香港的地方掠過。年少無知的我從未領略過颱風的威力，認為父親小題大做；但仍幫忙拿了一些必需品，我們一起住到工人房及廚房。

晚上十時五十分，七號風球掛起，風勢達烈風程度，橫瀾島更錄得每小時四十八海浬的陣風，呼嘯的風聲和雜物碰撞聲令我們徹夜難眠。早上四時十五分，九號風球懸掛，兩個小時後，十號風球掛起，溫黛距港只有五十英哩，直趨香港。更糟的是，風暴來到時正值天文大潮，維港的水位比正常潮漲還高出六呎。

我們徹夜未眠，瑟縮在住宅的後方，看著客廳已關上的門給吹得像彎柳，真擔心它能否撐得過去；突然傳來一聲玻璃碎裂的巨響，我們不知發生了什麼事，但亦不打算查看究竟。

溫黛的風眼早上近距離掠過長洲，一切轉趨平靜，給我們無限遐想，以為風暴已經過去....錯錯錯！風眼過後，風力再次增強並從另一方向吹襲，橫瀾島錄得超過時速八十海浬的陣風，中心附近更錄得九十五海浬。一小時後，溫黛開始遠離，六號風球取代了十號，然後再改掛三號。強風持續至九月二日，直到溫黛在中國大陸登陸為止，所有風球除下。

驚魂甫定，我們離開工人房及廚房，探個究竟客廳發生了甚麼事！眼前所見令我們大吃一驚。住宅兩側不見了，外牆，窗戶和露台全沒有了，只見到處瓦礫。厚重的中式羊毛地氈吸飽了水，重得沒法移動，沙發和椅子消失了。可幸我們來得及搬走檯燈，畫和一些小物件，而那些笨重的傢俱都隨風而去。濕了的東西花了數星期才乾透；重建客廳的期間，我們搬到酒店暫住。

風暴蹂躪香港，破壞令人難以想像，風災共造成一百三十人死亡，五十三人失蹤，無數的人無家可歸。小艇災情嚴重，571艘沉沒，726艘翻側，756艘受損，財物損失慘重。倒塌的山邊寮屋及竹棚，吹倒的電線，鐵皮屋頂及路牌，遍地玻璃碎片，滿目瘡痍。

走過的這段日子憂患與共，但無損我對香港的熱愛。歸來後與闊別多年的老朋友們重聚，日子也過得別具意義。時光荏苒，轉眼一甲子，放眼今天，倍覺歲月逝無蹤。

昔日故友多已離港，少數的仍不時緬懷昔日殖民地的時光。如果你曾身處其中，這書或許會令你勾起無限回憶；揭示昔日，對於年輕一代來說，更像走進一條時光隧道，舊事舊物，活現眼前。

一九四零年代末至五零年代的尖沙嘴，曾經是我多年的遊樂場；滄海桑田，此情此景已不復再。但這畢竟是香港及我人生中不可磨滅的部分，希望你翻閱這書的時候，也能感受到我腦海中對香港的這份回憶。

as a school for all nationalities (his father was Dutch) but after some negotiations it came to be known as the Kowloon British School for pupils from five to fifteen years of age.

There were several headmasters but the one who made the most impact was Franklin Nightingale (1916) whose far-sighted policy resulted in the formation of a Former Pupils Association and a request for donations for expansion. This resulted in the opening of Kowloon Junior School (KJS), thereby leaving Kowloon British School (KBS) as a purely secondary school; KBS continued to expand and in 1936 was relocated to its current site on Tin Kwong Road in Ho Man Tin in a new building and renamed the Central British School (CBS). At this time, Kowloon Junior School was operating from premises near the Kowloon Cricket Club on Cox's Road, but they were completely destroyed in the war.

When schools reopened in 1946, CBS was able to take in both juniors and seniors but by 1947 the numbers had increased so much that the La Salle Annex on the corner of La Salle Road and Boundary Street was taken over as the Kowloon Junior School and CBS became the senior school once more. It was at the school prize giving on 30th April 1948 that Governor Sir Alexander Grantham announced that the Central British School was to be renamed King George V School (KGV) and would be open to all nationalities.

One day while I was still at the junior school, we were playing marbles in the middle of the playground when we uncovered something metal. It turned out to be a bomb that had been dropped by the Japanese during the war. There was great excitement when we were duly evacuated from the school while the army attended to it, but to our disappointment it was a dud and never went off.

After the evacuation of women and children from Hong Kong in 1940, CBS had been set aside as a military hospital and used as such in December 1941 and later as a hospital for European POWs. Over the main hall can be seen the famous words of Winston Churchill: "Never in the field of human conflict…" The hospital housed around one hundred and thirty patients and had an operating theatre and an X-ray room. The clock tower (still there) was used as a chapel. Vegetable gardens were cultivated on parts of the playing field and the prisoners of war also created a putting green and a croquet lawn.

In 1949, I moved up to the senior school, which was already by then KGV, and I remained there until I left to go to boarding school in 1952. In the years since, I think many thousands of students and staff must have passed through its doors. The school's original 1902 site next door to St. Andrew's Church in Nathan Road, where I was christened, is now a heritage building.

I made many friends at school and one day after classes one of them asked me if I would like to go horseback riding. Always ready for a new adventure off I went to the Gun Club Army Barracks on Austin Road where there were ponies for hire. To this day I do not know how I paid for the ride because my pocket money of only one dollar a week was certainly not enough! However, I must have borrowed it expecting my parents to refund it.

We mounted our ponies and with a soldier escorting us we went off along Chatham Road towards Kowloon Tong. In those days Wylie Road only went as far as the turning to King's Park Flats and at that point there was no Queen Elizabeth Hospital or British Military Hospital but hills instead, which we proceeded to walk over on our sure-footed ponies. We continued to walk until we reached Waterloo Road, which had a nullah, a large storm water drain, running down the centre, reducing the road by a third of the width that it is today. Just as we approached the bridge a heavy locomotive went across and my pony bolted up Waterloo Road at full gallop. Not knowing how to stop I clung on for dear life until the pony finally ran out of steam by the China Light and Power Building at the junction with Argyle Street.

The other riders finally caught up with me and we continued at a sedate walk until we reached the end of Waterloo Road where Osborn Barracks are today. There was a very large open area of grass and red clay ground. The escorting soldier said we could canter around there but before I could get myself organised my pony shied and without warning I fell off into a large puddle of muddy red water.

I arrived home in my school uniform, covered in mud. I was very excited about my escapade, but my mother was furious with me for many reasons, not the least of which was that I had never been on a horse before and could have got badly injured galloping up the road. But as a ten-year-old I thought it was the greatest thing to have done. Later, I went on to learn how to ride properly at boarding school.

Communists and their aftermath

The year 1949 is one hard to forget. A communist victory in China was certain and thousands upon thousands of refugees flooded into Hong Kong – they came not only on foot overland, but also by train, plane and boat – rich and poor alike, all refugees.

With no housing available, many slept on the streets and began to build squatter huts on the hillsides, and these would frequently go up in smoke. But as Hong Kong began to recover from the war, more shops and factories opened up and poorly constructed buildings began to appear. It wasn't, however, until 1957 that one of the first low-cost housing estates was built in Wong Tai Sin, soon to be followed by many more. It was undoubtedly the hard work and resourcefulness of these dispossessed people that helped Hong Kong prosper in the post-war years.

In the summer of 1949, my father came home one day and told us that a friend was going on home leave and had offered us his flat on Hong Kong Island in Dina House, Duddell Street, for three months. I was over the moon because with the flat went a little Scottie dog named Jock. By then we had lived in the Peninsula for two years and my biggest – but impossible – wish was to have a dog. I couldn't get there fast enough, and I was so happy when I could take Jock to the grounds around St. John's Cathedral after school to play. But all too soon the three months were up and we had to return to the Pen. Alternative accommodation was still being constructed.

While we were living in Dina House, and so close to the Cathedral, school friends who were in the choir there suggested that I join, too. I had no idea if I could sing but I thought it was a good idea to try, so I attended the first Friday choir practice and was accepted; it helped perhaps that my parents were both Welsh! Choir practice for the young members of the choir was held at 4.30 p.m. and the adults came later after work when we had a full practice together. Between singing and waiting for the seniors we used to go up the Cathedral tower and sit on the wall looking down. It seemed that the door was never locked, but once we were discovered that was the end of our climbing the tower.

At Christmas, the whole choir used to go around singing carols at various places like Government House, Queen Mary Hospital and Ho Tung Gardens, Sir Robert Ho Tung's mansion on the Peak. At Sir Robert's we were all invited inside for drinks afterwards; the grown-ups had sherry and we had orange juice. Most of the adults did not finish a full glass and so when it was time to leave, I would dawdle behind and polish off most of the dregs. The servants thought it very amusing – and I left, a happy chorister.

By 1950, most of my friends whose parents were in government service had been allocated government quarters either at King's Park Flats in Kowloon, now redeveloped, or in Leighton Hill Flats on Hong Kong Island, and had left the hotel. I missed them and our escapades greatly.

We eventually moved out of the Peninsula hotel in early 1951 to a brand new flat in a brand new road named Kimberley Street. It ran parallel to the much bigger Kimberley Road and as the surface of the road was not yet tarred, friends and I would make a hole in the red clay and practise golf putting. Since there was no traffic it kept us occupied for several hours!

I will always remember the excitement I felt over being able to have my own room after nearly five years of living in one room with my parents in the hotel. But it didn't last

long as the following year my parents sent me to boarding school in the United Kingdom; class sizes in Hong Kong had got very large and my father thought I would benefit from more individual attention and a liberal curriculum. I missed Hong Kong and the fun and freedom I had had, but it was time to become serious about life.

In the intervening years the colony had already changed considerably. The flow of refugees from China had continued and the territory was well on its way to becoming a major manufacturing hub. The city was becoming prosperous.

At the time of my return, my parents were living in Waterloo Road, but in 1960 we moved into a two-storied apartment right behind Caritas in Boundary Street, Kowloon, and diagonally opposite Maryknoll Convent School. The flat was large with a balcony that ran along two of its sides and had a north-facing open view towards Lion Rock, and while living there I was to witness an extraordinary event. I had experienced many typhoons in my earlier years in Hong Kong, with little or no damage to our homes, but when infamous Typhoon Wanda struck in 1962 it was something very different.

Wanda had formed as a tropical depression in the Pacific at about 1,300 miles to the east-south-east of Hong Kong on 27th August 1962. It was moving in a west-north-westerly direction and by the following day was upgraded to a severe tropical storm. The circulation of the typhoon covered an area of about 1,000 miles and it continued to move towards the colony. By that second evening it was centred 400 miles east-south-east of Hong Kong and Number 1 signal was hoisted. The winds at this time were generally light to moderate but by early the next morning they were coming from the north and were freshening.

On 31st August, which was Liberation Day and a public holiday, Number 3 signal was hoisted. My father, with his knowledge of maritime weather, said we must move to the back of our flat and take some of our belongings with us. Being young and uninformed about the damage a bad typhoon could do, I thought these arrangements were excessive, but I helped with what was necessary and we all decamped to the amah's quarters and kitchen. The winds were still not that strong, but it was certain that Wanda would pass very close to us the next day.

At 10.50 p.m. Number 7 signal went up as the winds reached gale force with gusts of 48 knots at Waglan. We tried to sleep but the noise of the wind and things rattling around outside prevented this. At 4.15 a.m. Number 9 signal was hoisted and two hours later Number 10, when Wanda was only 50 miles away and heading straight for us.

Making the situation more dangerous, the arrival of the typhoon was going to coincide with a high tide; the tide in the harbour was expected to rise to more than six feet above normal.

We battened down at the far end of our flat spending a sleepless night watching the sitting room door, which was closed, bowing like a willow and wondering if it would hold. Suddenly there was a very loud bang followed by the sound of breaking glass. We had no idea what this was and we had no desire to leave our refuge to find out.

At mid-morning the eye of Wanda passed very close to Cheung Chau and all was calm, giving many the idea that

it was over… Wrong! The wind strength increased again with gusts exceeding 80 knots at Waglan Island and 95 at its centre. Finally, Wanda began to move away and the Number 10 signal was replaced by Number 6 in the afternoon, and then by Number 3. Strong winds persisted and it was not until 2nd September when Wanda made landfall in China that all signals were lowered.

What a shock we had when we left the safety of the kitchen and amah's room to investigate what had happened in our sitting room. Both sides of the apartment were gone: no walls, no windows, no balcony doors… and piles of bricks

everywhere. Our heavy Chinese wool carpet was saturated and impossible to move with its weight of water, and the sofa and chairs had vanished. Fortunately, we had had time to move our lamps and pictures and a lot of smaller items, never thinking for a moment that the heavy furniture would take off in the wind. It took weeks to dry everything out and many more to rebuild the sitting room, during which time we moved to a hotel.

The damage throughout the colony was unimaginable. One hundred and thirty people had been killed, fifty-three people were missing and no end of people made homeless. Small craft suffered badly with 571 sunk, 726 wrecked and 756 damaged. Destruction of property was extensive, especially among the squatter huts on the hillsides, with debris everywhere: the hillsides were covered with torn bamboo scaffolding, electrical wiring, sheets of iron roofing, sign boards and shattered glass.

While it was an extremely alarming experience to have lived through, it didn't diminish my love for Hong Kong. I was back with my friends whom I had not seen for many years and life took on another meaning. Here I am today, some sixty years later, and wonder where the years have gone.

Many of my friends who were here at the time have since left Hong Kong, but there are still a few who will recall that period in the colony. For those of you who were here, this will perhaps bring back nostalgic memories, and for the younger generation, I hope it will be an amusing and a surprising revelation.

Tsim Sha Tsui had been my playground for many years in the late 1940s and 1950s – unimaginable now – and it was a very special time in the history of Hong Kong and in my life. It is a history which I hope you will enjoy as you turn the pages of my memories of the Hong Kong I knew.

EPILOGUE

The establishment of the People's Republic of China in October 1949 meant that most westerners living in China had to leave. As a consequence, there were no western eye-witness accounts of what was happening there through the 1950s and 1960s. The main source of information was from escaping mainland refugees, and China, in the eyes of the outsider, began to take on an aura of mystique as a forbidden land.

Although in the early 1970s there was an unexpected rapprochement with the United States, it was more than a decade before foreigners were allowed into the country to meet ordinary Chinese in any numbers. So for almost thirty years, westerners in Hong Kong were shut out of this fabled land, separated from it by the Sham Chun River. Two strips of barbed-wire fencing and an area of no-man's land that lay between were constantly patrolled.

The politics of the time were such that few westerners actually wanted to go there, but most were curious as to what it was like. The border extended, as it still does, from Starling Inlet in the east to Deep Bay in the west, a distance of some thirty kilometres. Lok Ma Chau was a high point close to the western end from where it was possible to look over the green fields of the Frontier Closed Area, across the Sham Chun River and into the farmland to the north, and with a good pair of binoculars to pick out Chinese workers tending vegetable plots or meandering duck farms. Visiting it a decade after the war soon became a tradition. There was a certain element of voyeurism in all this and it was on the itinerary of almost every visitor in town.

The lookout at Lok Ma Chau was approached by a narrow road from San Tin at the top of which was a small parking area. A couple of stalls operated by Hakka women sold cold drinks well over the normal price, postcards and sundry souvenirs, between which one had to pass to reach the lookout itself.

One of the highlights of the visit was to take photographs of and with the posed Hakka women but this did not come free and one would be confronted with a sea of outstretched hands waiting for the money. Any attempt to photograph the women in their iconic fringed Hakka hats and distinct black work top and trousers without paying a predetermined fee was met with a stiff rebuke. For an extra coin or two, they would produce a long pipe and smoke as well. It was a habit which no doubt contributed to the deep wrinkles which defined their faces. These photo opportunities were all part of the experience.

Sheltered by shade-giving trees, the lookout provided a splendid 180-degree view into China and Deep Bay and offered another perfect backdrop for those one-of-a kind tourist photographs. Being able to say they had looked into China was a highlight of most visitors' Hong Kong experience.

But all this was set to change.

In the late 1970s, following China's "reform and opening-up", it was announced that Shenzhen on the north side of the Sham Chun River would become home to the country's first Special Economic Zone. No one in Hong Kong quite anticipated what was to follow and visiting Lok Ma Chau in the mid-to-late 1980s provided a considerable shock! That perfect backdrop of vegetable plots and duck farms had gone forever. In its place stood an enormous, and relentlessly expanding, concrete metropolis, its population now well in excess of 12 million!

Lok Ma Chau had lost its mystique! "Shopping in Shenzhen" became the new mantra and was to represent something of a watershed in Hong Kong's fortunes.

結語

一九四九年十月，中華人民共和國成立，意味著大部分住在中國的西方人要離開。結果是沒有任何西方國家能目擊並描述，一九五零年及六零年代在中國所發生的事情。有關中國的信息主要來自逃出來的大陸難民，而在這些國家的眼中，中國猶如散發著神秘光環的禁地。

儘管在一九七零年代初，中，美兩國令人意想不到的恢復友好關係，可是外國人卻在十年後才被允許到訪中國，與平民百姓接觸。所以有將近三十年時間，深圳河彼岸居港的西方人被拒諸這片聞名土地的門外。分隔兩地的兩道鐵絲網牆和中間的無人地帶，就有執法人員不斷巡邏。

基於當時的政治環境，實際上亦只有少數西方人想到中國去，大部分是出於好奇。邊境延綿三十多公里，從東邊的沙頭角至西邊的后海灣。接近西邊盡頭是地勢較高的落馬洲，從那裡可以俯瞰邊境禁區的翠綠田野，以及深圳河以北的一片農地，在一副好的望遠鏡協助下，更能一覽無遺地看到農夫在打理菜田和那些蜿蜒的養鴨場。戰後的十年，在落馬洲北望大陸成了傳統，這肯定是有偷窺的心態，但卻成為很多城中遊客的旅行路線。

從新田的一條狹窄小路前往，走到最高處，便可到達落馬洲觀景台旁的一個小停車場。往觀景台必須經過的路上，有幾家由客家女子經營的攤檔，售賣一些比正常價高的冷飲，明信片和各式各樣的紀念品。來到這裡其中一個重要環節，便是拍下擺著各種姿勢的客家女子的照片或與她們合照，這當然不是免費的，她們跟着便會蜂擁而上伸手向你索取金錢。若你嘗試拍下頭戴有帽簷的客家涼帽，身穿獨特的黑色衫褲的客家女子的照片，而又沒有付予指定的費用，定必受到她們嚴斥。但只要多加一兩塊錢，她們更會拿着煙槍吸煙供你拍照，無疑這習慣為她們臉上添加深深的皺紋，但這些拍照機會也算是體驗的一部份。

在樹蔭下，從觀景台看到的是一百八十度景觀的中國和后海灣，為遊客提供一個完美的背景拍攝獨一無二的照片。在很多訪港遊客的體驗中，最精彩的部份可說是能一窺中國。

但這一切都將改變。

一九七零年代末，隨著中國「改革開放」，深圳河以北的深圳宣告成立第一個特別經濟區。在香港沒有人能預測接下來會發生甚麼；原本有著菜田與鴨場的完美背景永遠消失，取而代之的是一個龐大，不斷發展，不折不扣的大都會，給一九八零年代中後期到訪落馬洲的遊客大吃一驚，今天的她人口已超過一千二百萬！

落馬洲已失去了它的神秘感！「深圳購物」成為了新的口頭禪，一個標誌著香港命運的轉捩點。

SIGHTS AND SCENES OF EVERYDAY LIFE
日常生活的見聞及風貌

RICKSHAWS
人力車

Apart from the few single-decker buses that survived the war, the most popular form of transport was the rickshaw. If the weather was fine, the top cover was down; if it was wet, the top was up and an oil cloth curtain was hooked in the front to keep you dry. The rickshaw coolie was dressed accordingly. If you knew the system, and most locals did, you negotiated the fare before embarking, otherwise you would sure to be overcharged. Many people saw this mode of transport as an inhuman way of travelling and tried to avoid it. But doing so was not a kindness as it meant that the rickshaw coolie missed out on a day's wage; it was his only source of income and he needed the passengers.

除了幾輛在戰後倖存的單層巴士，那時候最流行的交通工具就是人力車。晴天的日子，帳蓬會褪下來；雨天的日子，車伕會拉起帳蓬，在前面掛上油布簾遮擋雨水，以免濺濕客人，車伕自己也會披上簑衣。本地人一般都懂得規矩，出發前必定會與車伕議好車資，否則一定會被多收。很多人覺得拉人力車是對車伕不人道，儘量避免乘坐；但這反而害苦了車伕，因為他們正是靠每天的車資收入維持生計。

LADIES WITH BOUND FEET
紮腳的老婦

In the 1950s, a few old ladies could still be seen struggling along Nathan Road on their tiny bound feet. Now in their eighties, they would have been born in the 1860s when the binding of feet was legal and considered necessary for the better class. It was a cruel and painful practice, but it was believed that without it young women would never find a husband. The foot binding began when the girl was around four years old. The toes were forced underneath the foot with just the big toe left out and a ten-foot bandage was wrapped around the toes and tightened every day. This process usually took about two years during which time flesh often rotted and fell off as did some of the toes.

The crippling custom of foot binding was started in China in the tenth century and was supposedly done to prevent women from straying, but it continued because men found the "golden lily" foot, measuring no more than five inches, both attractive and erotic and the epitome of feminine beauty. The practice was officially banned in China in the early part of the twentieth century but continued in some areas such as Shanxi and in remote rural areas of provinces like Yunnan until the 1950s. Missionaries had been early campaigners in the late nineteenth century against this unnecessary cruelty, but it took the communists coming to power in 1949 to finally stigmatise the practice.

直至一九五零年代初期，偶爾仍可見到幾位紮腳的老婦，沿着彌敦道蹣跚而行。她們年約八十多歲，大概生於一八六零年代的清朝；那時上流社會的女性紮腳是合法及認為有需要的，雖然這是一種殘忍而且令人痛苦的行為，但普遍認為沒有紮腳的女性很難嫁出去。女性一般四歲開始便紮腳，除了拇趾以外，其餘的腳趾都被強行向下屈曲，然後用繃帶把腳趾和腳掌牢牢包紮，這樣維持約兩年，沒有一天放鬆，防止足部繼續發育。在這期間腳掌的肌肉因長期包紮而潰爛，腳趾也會跟着脫落。

紮腳這種陋俗始於十世紀，原先目的是希望把婦女禁於閨房，但發展下去却被視為女性的病態美，認為小足的女性具吸引力和性感，以及凸顯女性美；更有「金蓮」之說 － 即是足部不長於五寸。有教會人士在十九世紀末已發起運動，反對這種不必要的殘忍行為。二十世紀初中國正式禁止紮腳，最終共產黨於一九四九年掌權後聲討這行為，但在山西和偏遠的省份如雲南，仍繼續至一九五零年代才結束。

FIRECRACKERS
放炮竹(燒炮仗)

Celebrations of any sort, such as for the Lunar New Year, a wedding, the opening of a new building or other important occasion, were considered incomplete without plenty of firecrackers to ward off evil spirits. It was not unusual to see strings of red crackers as long as thirty feet or more attached to the top of a building and lit from below. The strings could take up to half an hour to completely burn out with a resulting lot of noise and gunpowder smoke, to say nothing of the amount of red paper left in the road. Just before Chinese New Year, all these firecrackers would be on sale in the shops and we would buy as many as we could with what little pocket money we had. Our biggest thrill was to light a cracker, put an empty tin can on it and watch it fly up into the air as the cracker exploded. Eventually in 1967, firecrackers were banned as an illegal use of gunpowder and this ban, although not always obeyed, is still in force today.

不管是慶祝農曆新年，新大廈落成，婚禮或一些重要場合，沒有燃放炮竹來驅趕邪靈，就好像欠缺了什麼似的。我們不時看見有長達三十呎的鞭炮從樓頂吊到地面，人們就在地面那頭用火燃點，隨之而來就是劈啪巨響和漫天硝煙，這樣長的炮竹可燃燒約半小時，燃燒過後滿地紅色紙屑。農曆新年前夕，到處的商店都在售賣炮竹，我們就傾盡那丁點的零用錢去購買。小朋友們最感興奮的就是把小枚燃點的炮竹，放進掏空的煉奶罐，反過來蓋在

地上，爆炸的威力把罐子彈上半空。一九六七年暴動，有人利用炮竹的火藥來製造炸彈，自此政府宣布禁止燃放炮竹，一直維持至今，偶爾仍會有人偷偷的放。

THE ROYAL OBSERVATORY – Signal Hill
皇家香港天文台 — 訊號山

The observatory tower, which still stands today, was built in 1907 and named Blackhead's Hill, although it was more commonly known as Signal Hill. It was heightened in 1928 to give a better view for the ships in the harbour, and to accommodate the time ball. Both the time ball and the typhoon signal mast were originally installed at the Marine Police Headquarters at the corner of Canton Road and Salisbury Road but were moved to the new site in 1907.

This hill is right in the middle of Tsim Sha Tsui behind what is now the Sheraton Hotel, and was visible for miles around. If a typhoon was approaching, you only had to look to Signal Hill to see what was happening. This system had been designed mainly for seafarers so that junks, sampans and other small craft could take shelter in the typhoon anchorage in Causeway Bay or Yau Ma Tei. Initially there were ten signals, but this was eventually cut down to eight and still used now, four of which are actually directional. Signals 5 to 8 were replaced by four number 8s (NW, SW, NE and SE) and the rest remained. At night these signals were shown by three vertical lights of white and green according to the number with red added to number 10, but these lights are no longer used. The numbers themselves are still used but the signals are no longer hoisted.

For many years, typhoons were traditionally given girls' names such as Rose, Mary and Wanda, but like much else, these were phased out and a range of names are now used.

建於一九零七年的天文台訊號塔，今天仍矗立在一座叫黑頭角(普遍稱為訊號山) 的小山崗上。為了讓港內的船隻更容易看見報時球，一九二八年的時候把它加高至現時的高度。報時球和立体風球訊號原先是安置在廣東道與梳士巴利道交界的水警總部，一九零七年才搬到現在的地方。

那小山崗位於尖沙嘴市中心，就在今天喜來登酒店後面，方圓數哩可見。每當颱風來臨，你只要抬頭望向訊號山，便知最新情況。這套系統的設計，主要是對港內作業的小艇，舢舨和帆船發出警告，好讓他們在颱風來臨前，駛回銅鑼灣或油麻地避風塘避風。最早期的時候共有十個風球訊號，最終減至現在的八個，其中四個是同等級，只代表不同風向。五號至八號風球分別由四個代表不同風向(西北，西南，東北，東南)的八號風球取代，其它的維持不變。夜間訊號由白色和綠色組合的三個垂直燈號顯示，而十號風球的燈號則是紅綠紅，燈號多年前已取消，只剩下訊號繼續懸掛。

多年來，颱風傳統上是以女性名字來命名，如露絲，瑪麗和温黛等。時移勢易，很多名字已逐步淘汰，今天颱風的名字變得多元化。

No. 1
一號風球

No. 3
三號風球

No. 8 NE
八號東北

No. 8 NW
八號西北

No. 8 SE
八號東南

No. 8 SW
八號西南

No. 9
九號風球

No. 10
十號風球

JUNKS AND SAMPANS
帆船和舢舨

As trade increased and Hong Kong began to flourish as a mercantile centre in the Far East, and long before containerisation came into being, junks and sampans were used to unload goods from ships anchored in the harbour. These were the genuine junks that travelled under sail and they could be seen with the waterline almost up to the deck as they ploughed down the harbour with a full load. They made a magnificent sight with their rust red sails and teakwood hulls, but in the name of progress the sails soon disappeared, and the junks became mechanised. Speed was money. The occasional old and rather worn Chinese sailing junk could still be seen in Hong Kong waters into the 1970s, but as China "opened up", they too became a sight of the past.

隨着貿易開始蓬勃，香港成為遠東商業中心，但距離貨櫃化還是遙不可及的時候，替停泊在維港的輪船裝卸貨物的重任，便落在帆船和舢舨身上。滿載貨物的真正帆船，航行時載浮載沉，船身水位很多時候高達甲板；銹紅色的帆配以柚木造的船身，揚帆港內，煞是壯觀。假進步之名，舢舨很快便消失，帆船也變成機械化，畢竟速度就是金錢。一九七零年代，我們還偶爾看到一些破舊的中國帆船在港海航行，隨着中國開放，它們都成為歷史光景。

FERRY SERVICE – Cross Harbour
渡海小輪

The first records showing that a ferry service was in operation are from 1888, the ferries owned by the Kowloon Ferry Company. By the turn of the century, ownership had been taken over by a Parsee called Norabjee Nowrojee and the business named the Star Ferry Company. Each ferry had the suffix "Star" i.e. Morning Star, Twinkling Star etc. in its name and it crossed back and forth between Kowloon and Hong Kong.

At more or less the same time, another enterprising man named Lau Tak Lo bought five wooden boats and turned them into ferries and so began the services of the Yau Ma Tei Ferry Company. Later he added bigger ferries to his fleet which could take vehicles on board, enabling motorised transport to cross the harbour. Waiting in your car on a hot summer's day at Jordan Road pier could be very uncomfortable as there was no air conditioning in cars at that time and the only relief was the Dairy Farm ice cream man when he came by. Much as they have might wished for a tunnel, with car queues getting longer, no one really dreamt at that time that one day we would drive under the harbour to get to the other side, let alone have a choice of three routes. The Jordan Road pier has now been lost to reclamation and vehicular ferries made redundant.

During the war all the ferries were grounded for three and a half years (or had been sunk), leaving them in a state of disrepair when war ended. When ferry services resumed in 1946, fares were retained at their pre-war level. Adults paid twenty cents to travel on Star Ferry's first-class deck and ten cents to travel third class. It was the protests that resulted from the 25 per cent raise in ferry fares in 1966 that are said to have encouraged the unforgettable territory-wide communist-inspired riots of the following year.

有記錄的渡海小輪服務於一八八八年開始營運,渡輪由九龍渡海小輪公司擁有。踏入二十世紀,公司易手予一位叫諾爾布·納羅吉的拜火教徒,易名天星小輪公司,每艘船的名字皆以「星」字結尾,如曉星,熒星等,來往維港兩岸。差不多同時,有一位中國商人劉德譜購入五艘木船,將它改裝成渡海小輪,並以油麻地小輪公司的名義投入服務。其後他更購入較大型可以搭載汽車的渡輪,成為當時汽車可以渡海的唯一途徑。炎炎夏日的佐敦道碼頭,呆坐沒有冷氣的汽車內的滋味叫人難受,唯一的消暑辦法,就是等待賣牛奶公司雪糕的小販出現。正當汽車在大排長龍等候過海的時候,大概沒有人會夢想到將來能駕車在水下橫渡維港,更遑論今天有三條海底隧道可供選擇。佐敦道碼頭今天已經填海,而汽車渡輪則變得多餘了。

二戰期間直至一九四六年,渡海小輪全部停航,三年半的停駛令大部份船隻都失修。渡海小輪服務在一九四六年恢復,票價跟戰前的一樣不變,成人頭等兩毫,三等一毫。一九六六年天星小輪加價五仙,翌年就引發起據說是由左派煽動,令人難忘的六七全港大暴動。

TRAFFIC POLICEMEN
交通警察

It was a few years before Hong Kong was able to control the ever-increasing Kowloon traffic by installing traffic lights on the main thoroughfare of Nathan Road. At first, the traffic was controlled by a policeman who stood in the middle of a junction, stopping traffic one way, and starting it from another, often forgetting whose turn it was, and this would end in a cacophony of horns as drivers got impatient. At complicated junctions, the policeman could not always be seen as he moved from one section to the next, and things often got out of hand. The addition of a raised pagoda not only placed the policeman in clear view but also gave him shelter from the midday sun. These pagodas were eventually used all over Hong Kong and Kowloon until the advent of the red, yellow and green traffic lights.

在香港還沒能力安裝交通燈控制交通以前，在一些交通日益繁忙的主幹道如彌敦道，路上行駛的車輛都是依賴警察來指揮。他站在馬路交匯處的中央，截停一邊的車輛，放行另一邊；間有出錯，便換來欠耐性的司機響號抗議。在縱橫交錯的十字路口，交通警員忙於應付四方八面而來的車輛，難免有時會手忙腳亂。後來有了昇高寶塔狀的交通崗，警察站在上面除可居高臨下，視野廣濶，還可免於日曬雨淋，在紅黃綠三色的交通燈發明之前，這些交通崗遍佈港九。

THE CLOG SHOP
屐店

One shop that I loved as a child was the wooden clog shop along Peking Road a few shops away from the Peking Market stalls. I used to pester my mother to stop so that I could look at the brightly painted soles in the hope that she would buy me a pair. Eventually she succumbed and I duly sat in the chair to have the strap nailed on over my foot for the perfect fit. Most of the amahs wore these wooden clogs and there was a higher, heavier type made of plain wood for market workers. The sound of clop, clop, clop as they walked along remains memorable.

我兒時最喜歡的其中一家商店，便是北京道街市附近的一家賣木屐的店舖。每當路過我總愛纏着母親停下來，好讓我飽看顏色鮮艷的木屐，期望她也能買我一對。她終於屈服在我的苦纏之下，我於是坐在椅上，讓師傅(鞋匠)量度我雙足的大小，為木屐釘上合適的背帶。大部份的媽姐(女傭)都愛穿木屐，另外一種木底較厚重的屐，則是專為在街市工作的工人而造。那種走起路來「咯，咯，咯」的響聲，至今難忘！

FUNERALS
殯葬儀式

When a person died at home, custom required that the body should not be carried out through the front door. A bamboo ramp or staircase had to be constructed from a window or verandah on an upper floor or wherever appropriate to enable the coffin or body to leave without it passing through the building. This was to foil the evil spirits and bring peace to the house; it was also a fact that most of the time the coffin was far too big to go through a normal door. Mourners would also use this improvised exit.

Because there were very few cars in the 1950s, funeral processions could often be seen progressing on foot towards the funeral parlours or burial grounds, led by a band playing very loud music to frighten away the spirits and ghosts. The size of the procession was an indication of the wealth of the deceased and often there were as many as six bands all playing different tunes. That was enough to frighten any ghost away! The main mourners, dressed in white with white sackcloth hoods over their heads, walked behind the first band. It was not unusual to hire professional mourners who would wail and cry as they walked along. Sometimes the mourners would be surrounded by a white screen so as not to be seen. Behind them would be the hearse containing the coffin adorned with flowers and a portrait of the deceased, followed by more bands and mourners. The funeral procession of Sir Robert Ho Tung that wound through Central on 2nd May 1956 was a prime example of such a grandiose occasion.

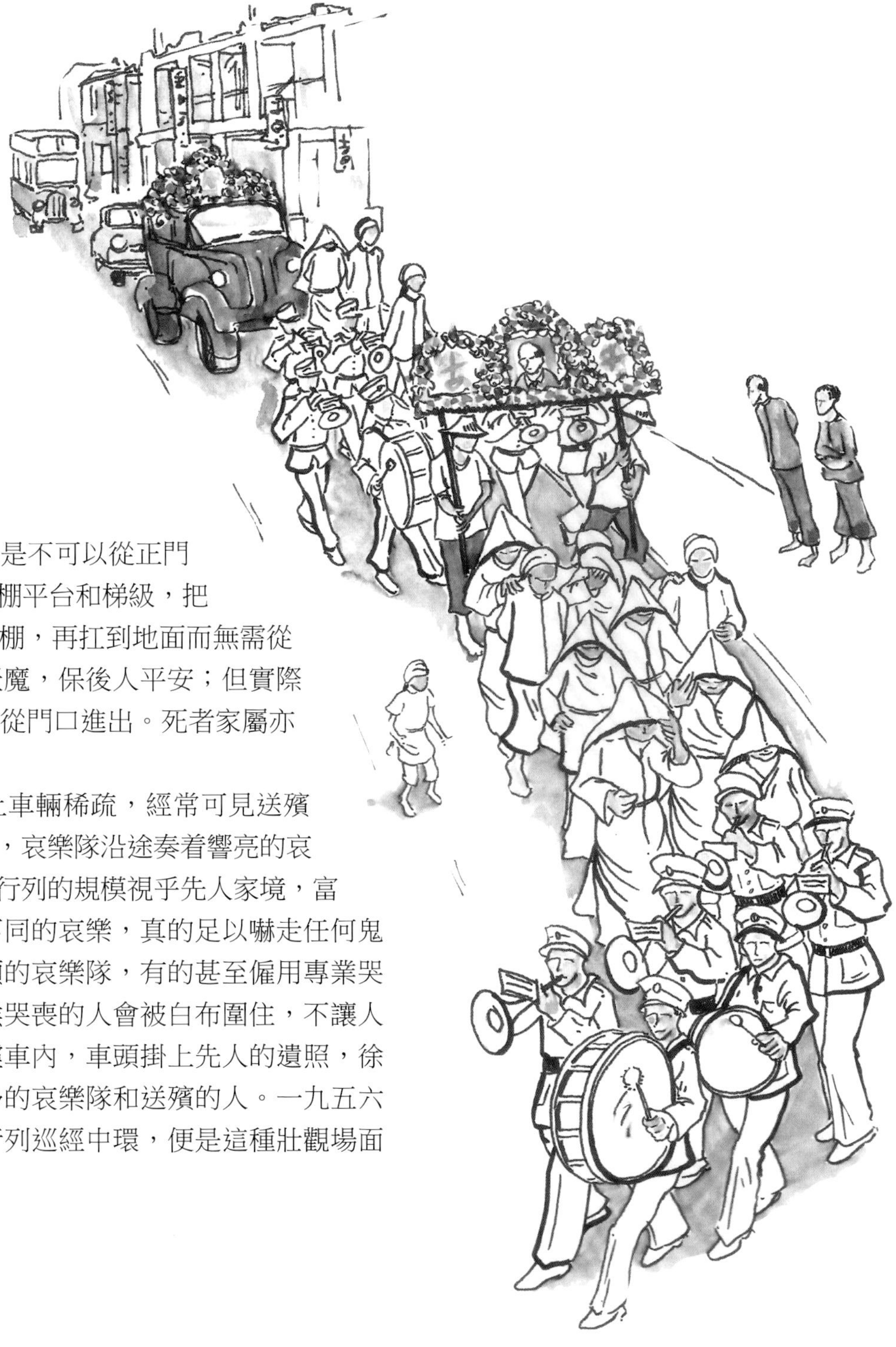

當有人在家中離世，習俗上遺體是不可以從正門
扛出去。因此需要在街上搭起竹棚平台和梯級，把
遺體或棺木從窗口或陽台送到竹棚，再扛到地面而無需從
樓宇內走過。此舉據說是驅走妖魔，保後人平安；但實際
來說是因為棺木過大，根本無法從門口進出。死者家屬亦
有使用這出口。

　　由於一九五零年代的香港街上車輛稀疏，經常可見送殯
行列在街上遊行至殯儀館或墳場，哀樂隊沿途奏着響亮的哀
樂，用以驅走魔鬼與靈魂。送殯行列的規模視乎先人家境，富
裕的有多至六隊哀樂隊，奏着不同的哀樂，真的足以嚇走任何鬼
怪！孝子賢孫披麻帶孝緊隨領頭的哀樂隊，有的甚至僱用專業哭
喪的人，沿途哀泣嚎哭。有時候哭喪的人會被白布圍住，不讓人
看見。鮮花伴着的棺木安放在靈車內，車頭掛上先人的遺照，徐
徐跟在後面，靈車後面就是更多的哀樂隊和送殯的人。一九五六
年五月二日，何東爵士的送殯行列巡經中環，便是這種壯觀場面
的表表者。

CHINESE-STYLE CLOTHING
中國傳統服裝

One of the things I miss most is seeing graceful Chinese women wearing the elegant cheong sam. No one in the world can wear that dress like the Asian woman. Every now and then the style would change slightly but generally it remained much the same. Sometimes the collar, which was stiffened, would be three inches high and looked uncomfortable in the summer heat. At other times it would be half the height. The slits on the sides of the dress were normally about a foot or more long on an ankle-length dress or just a few inches on the shorter ones, but this mainly came and went with the fashion of the time. It was a sad change when this elegant garment began to be worn less routinely, but then, the dress was not really practical for the busy working woman since the size of her step was restricted by the narrowness of the skirt. So, the cheong sam gradually disappeared and gave way to a more casual western-style dress. Although the cheong sam is no longer commonly worn, it has not disappeared completely and there is always the possibility of a revival.

When I was born, I was looked after by a baby amah, and later my parents had another amah who worked as a cook and cleaner. She came to us from China and did not have a birth certificate nor did she know how old she was.

She became part of our family and stayed with us for thirty-five years, in spite of the fact that she could not speak any English and my mother could not speak Cantonese. I was always amused listening to the two conversing about what to have for dinner. Ah Mui, as she was known, wore the samfu, which consisted of a high-necked white top and black trousers, and her hair, which had never been cut from the time she was born, was down to her knees and plaited in a queue or pig tail. She wore the typical amah attire.

The traditional men's attire was a suit made from a soft, shiny black cloth known as pongee. These suits were fashionable and very cool in the summer. The trousers were made very large around the waist so that they could be folded double in the front and tied and the jackets had a Chinese-style collar and Chinese buttons (frogs) down the front. Men mostly wore the soft Chinese black cloth shoe, which slipped on with no laces or straps.

It looked a much cooler and more comfortable outfit than that worn by men today.

其中一樣最讓我懷念的就是穿着優雅長衫(旗袍)的中國女性,全世界沒有誰比亞洲女性穿得更好看。長衫的款式雖間有些微修改,但設計基調不變。衣領一般為三吋高的企領,炎夏時候令人感覺不舒服,但有些款式又只有一半高。兩側的開义高度主要跟隨當時的時尚,衫身長至足踝的,义的高度有一呎多;衫身短的則只有數吋高。令人傷感的是長衫不再成為民間女性的日常衣著,但想到修身的設計而令女性蓮步姍姍,對於今天繁忙的職業女性來說,確實又不合時宜。隨着長衫逐漸淡出,西方的休閒服飾代之而興;但誰又敢說潮流不會復興。

我出生以後是由褓姆媽姐負責照顧,後來又多來了一位媽姐,專門負責煮飯和打掃清潔。她來自中國,由於沒有出世紙,自己也不知道年紀多大;她伴隨我家三十五年,儼如家中一份子。她不懂半句英語,而我媽也不諳廣東話,每當聽她倆商議晚餐餐單的時候,真是充滿娛樂性。她叫「阿梅」,穿著我們叫「衫褲」的白色高企領上衣和黑長褲,留有一頭及膝長髮,出生以來從沒修剪,長髮結紮成髻或繞成辮子,典型媽姐裝扮。

男仕唐裝是用布面光亮的黑膠綢造成的時尚套裝,夏天穿著感覺涼快。長褲腰圍造得濶大,需要在前面摺起兩層,然後用腰帶紮緊;上衣是中式的企領和對襟布鈕(蝌蚪狀)。他們大多穿著蹬入式的中式軟布鞋,沒有鞋繩或橫帶。

這種衣著看來比今天的男士服裝來得涼快和舒適。

FARMERS
農夫

If you were lucky enough to know someone with a car, a drive around the New Territories on a Sunday was always a great treat. There were no road tunnels through the mountains, just the one for the trains, so the only way to the New Territories was along Nathan Road and then round by the reservoir and past the fishing village of Shatin. From there you could drive on to Tai Po Market, then Fanling and on westwards to Yuen Long and Castle Peak. The whole journey could be done leisurely and with no traffic jams.

If you were there in the late afternoon, you could not fail to be aware of the dreadful smell that permeated the air as you drove along. It was the time for farmers to water their vegetables and human excrement was the formula. No commercial fertilisers were available so what better way to get rid of the human waste! If you were game enough to buy these vegetables – and there were few alternatives – it

was vitally important to wash them thoroughly in potassium permanganate to kill the bacteria. We did not eat locally grown watermelons for many years because of the presence of cholera in Hong Kong, which in 1946 claimed some 240 lives. However, this precautionary practice did not spare me the painful six-monthly jabs of the government's mass anti-cholera inoculation drives, despite my repeated protests.

Shatin was known as the Emperor's Rice Bowl. From one end of the Shatin valley to the other there were rice paddies as far as the eye could see. The lush green shoots were planted by hand and during the seasonal rains of July and August flourished into fully grown rice ears. Looking up towards the Kowloon foothills one could see two famous landmarks, Amah Rock and Lion Rock, both of which can still be seen today but building development and afforestation mean they are not quite as obvious and outstanding as they were.

Almost in the middle of these extensive paddy fields and within view of Amah Rock was a small hill on which stood the Shatin Babies' Home run by the extraordinarily dedicated English woman, Miss Mildred Dibden. She had established a Home in Fanling in 1936 for the growing number of abandoned babies, mainly girls, and when the Japanese soldiers arrived from across the border at the beginning of the war, its children and staff were brutally treated. She and her staff valiantly continued to care for the children during the war despite great deprivation. After repatriation leave in 1945, during when the Home was managed by another charity, Miss Dibden returned in 1946 and later set up her own new Home in Shatin for foundlings with her emphasis on "family". It was funded mainly by local community contributions.

Not only in Shatin but all along the roadsides of the New Territories the new season's crop of rice and rice straw was cut and dried along the paths. In order to have a continuous crop of rice, the paddies were prepared at different times so that while one area was being cut, another paddy was being ploughed, ready to plant the young green shoots. The ploughing was done by a man guiding a water buffalo, the planting was mainly carried out by Hakka women, so too the cutting and drying. It is difficult to believe that rice was once grown where all the high-rise blocks stand today. The Hakka originated from the north of China and over centuries settled in large numbers in South China. They were characterised by their wide fringed hats and black clothing.

如果你有幸認識有汽車的朋友，週日環遊新界倒是不錯的享受。那時只有一條供火車通過，而沒有供汽車行走的隧道，駕車到新界的唯一途徑就是沿彌敦道走，繞過九龍水塘及通過沙田的漁村，繼續往北走可到大埔墟及粉嶺，西行則可前往元朗及青山(今天的屯門)，全程可輕鬆完成而不愁堵車。

如果黃昏時駕車途經那裏，你絕不可能錯過那瀰漫空氣中的難聞氣味，因為正是農夫澆水施肥的時間，肥料就是人類的排泄物，那時候沒有化學肥料，這樣就正好解決了處理排泄物的問題。假若你準備購買這些選擇不多的蔬菜，最重要是用高錳酸鉀徹底洗淨及殺菌。一九四六年的時候，霍亂曾奪去了二百四十人的性命，政府因此推行大現模預防霍亂措施；我雖老大不願意，但仍免不了要接受為期六個月的防疫注射。因霍亂流行的關係，我們也多年沒有進食本地產的西瓜。

沙田過去被稱為皇帝的飯碗，沙田河谷的兩端，

極目滿是稻田。農夫彎身插秧，一片青蔥，經過七，八月份雨水的滋養，禾苗長成茁壯的稻米。朝九龍方向的山麓上望，可見兩座著名的地標 — 望夫石和獅子山，它們仍 立那裏，隨着周圍建築物的發展和綠化，今非昔比，風采漸失。

就在一片稻田的中央，距望夫石不遠的一個小山崗上，有一所「沙田育嬰院」，它是由一位很傑出的英國女性狄美蘭女士經營。一九三六年，隨着棄嬰的數目日增，她在粉嶺建立了一所育嬰院，接收被遺棄的嬰兒，主要是女嬰。戰爭初期，日軍越過邊境進入香港，育嬰院的兒童和職員均受到日軍的粗暴對待，雖然物資短缺，她和職員們仍勇敢地照顧嬰兒。當一九四五年，狄女仕被遣送回英國期間，育嬰院由另一慈善團體管理。一九四六年她重臨香港，在沙田獨自創辦棄嬰院，特別強調這是一個「家」，這個家的經費主要來自本地社會捐助。

從沙田至新界沿途兩旁，放滿剛收割的穀和稻草在曬晾。為確保全年都有稻米收成，農夫都會在不同時間和地方交錯插秧，務求這邊收割，那邊插秧。男人牽着水牛肩負犁田的重擔；插秧，收割和晒穀則大多由客家女人負責。令人難以想像的是，今天高樓大廈林立的地方過去竟是稻田。客家人源自中國北方，經過世代流徙，大部份定居於中國南方，黑色衣著和戴寬邊帽是他們的特色。

BUILDING CONSTRUCTION
建屋

After the war when building reconstruction was badly needed to get Hong Kong back on its feet, there was a great shortage of men to do the labouring work. Teams of bricklayers were then supported by Hakka women who were strong and tough. They were employed to carry heavy loads of bricks and sand, which they transported in baskets attached to each end of a bamboo pole and supported on their shoulders. They were fearless of the narrow bending planks they climbed as they made their way up several floors; they were perfectly balanced. There were no safety belts or hard hats and they just got on with the job.

Many a time I would see very pregnant women struggling up the planks and wondered if they would make it. I was told that they often had the baby on site and then went back to work.

"Maternity leave" in those days could mean an empty rice bowl.

戰後香港有大量建築物需要重建，令她重拾舊觀，但男性勞工卻甚為缺乏。由於客家女人強壯和刻苦，砌磚工人們的工作多由她們來支援。她們肩擔一根大竹杆，兩端掛着一個裝滿沉重的磚頭和沙泥的藤籃，無懼窄長軟彎的木板，往來於各樓層之間，平衡力驚人。她們沒有佩戴安全帶或安全帽，只顧默默工作。

我多次見到懷孕的女人竭力游走於木板上，驚訝她們怎可做到。有人告訴我，她們經常在工地誕下嬰兒後，隨即返回工作。

畢竟在那個年頭，產假即等於沒飯吃。

SHOE SHINE
擦鞋

With no homes to go to and sometimes no parents either, many children, often as young as six years old and often orphans, turned to shoe shining for a living. They would follow potential customers from street to street pulling at their clothes and saying, "Shoeshine, shoeshine, no mama, no papa, no whisky soda" until you agreed to the fifty cents they would charge. They each had their own box on which the customer rested one foot at a time. Pieces of cardboard were pushed into the shoes to protect the socks from the polish and the boy worked hard to get a mirror shine, even on old shoes! This event could take place anywhere on a pavement without fear of being knocked over. There are few pavements nowadays that offer enough space for someone to stand for fifteen minutes to have his shoes polished.

一群無家可歸或是孤兒的兒童，有些年紀小至六歲，被逼在街頭擦鞋謀生。每當蹺到有潛質的客人，他們就會跟隨數條街，拉着他們的衣服說：「擦鞋，擦鞋，沒有媽，沒有爸，沒有威士忌梳打」，讓你願意付五毫讓他擦鞋為止。他們各自有自己的擦鞋箱，客人一只腳踏在箱上，足踝四周圍上咭紙，以防弄髒襪子，他們努力的擦，舊鞋也變得鏡子般亮！今天的行人道行人熙來攘往，你還能想像如過去般的，能有足夠空間讓你站在那裏花十五分鐘擦鞋嗎？

THE INVISIBLE MENDER
神乎奇技的縫補師傅

Clothes, especially woollen ones, and ladies' silk nylon stockings, if available, were very expensive after the war so a tear or a "ladder" in a stocking would have to be repaired rather than the stocking discarded. It was a case of "a stitch in time, saves nine" and the garment was rushed off to the little lady who sat on the corner of Mody Road and Nathan Road who would make an invisible repair and have the item ready by the next day. It was the most amazing work ever seen and indeed, it was invisible. When the customer collected the garment, the mending lady would point to where the tear or hole had been, and it was invariably impossible to see it. Not only did she repair stockings but any type of woven material that was torn or damaged. As no one bothers to repair such things these days, the art of invisible mending has almost disappeared from our streets.

戰後初期，羊毛製的衣服與女性尼龍絲襪供應緊張，縱有亦昂貴；絲襪遇有破損或走線，都會寧補莫棄。本着「及時補一對，省九對」的想法，破損的襪子會被趕快交到小個子婦人的手上，她就坐

在麼地道與彌敦道轉角的地方，襪子翌日便補好，她通常會給你指看破損的部位，但似乎不易察覺，不着痕跡。除了絲襪外，任何梳織物料的衣服也能補。今天物資充裕，沒有人再想到會修補破衣服，神乎奇技的縫補工藝亦絕跡於街頭。

THE KNIFE SHARPENER
磨刀師傅

Over the years Hong Kong has lost so many useful tradespeople who gave a service to the community, one being the knife sharpener who would call out "mor gau tsien charn do" in a tone that everyone recognised as he went from house to house sharpening knives and scissors. He carried his wooden trestle over his shoulder and set up shop right there at the front of the building, sitting on the trestle and rubbing the various knives, cleavers and scissors on a special stone till they were dangerously sharp.

Where would one get a knife sharpened today? Knife sharpening is a dwindling trade, and if you don't have your own kitchen whetstone, there are still a few masters offering their skill in some of the older neighbourhoods.

這些年來，香港失去了很多有專門技藝，為社會提供非一般服務的人，磨刀師傅就是其中之一。他們用人們熟識的聲調高叫：「磨鉸剪劏刀」，挨門逐戶替人打磨刀剪。他們揹著木製工具箱，就在樓宇前面擺開架步，坐在工具箱上，拿出磨刀石，把客人交來的生果刀，切肉刀和鉸剪磨得閃爍鋒利。

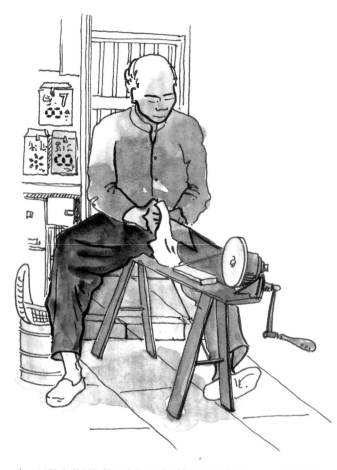

weight at the end and a small metal tray holding the fish. It was always taken to the nearest, but highest (cattie) weight before the price was announced. As more supermarkets and fish stalls began to open in Hong Kong, people like this disappeared from the streets and the atmosphere of the old Orient gradually diminished.

These were the people and characters who made life as it was in everyday Hong Kong in the 1950s.

聽到高聲叫「賣魚」，便知道赤柱來的婦人又有鮮魚販賣；挑好你要的魚，她便給你量一下多重。用的並非我們常見的量具，而是只有一根木杆，一根繩子，一端是秤陀，另一端是用來盛魚的小鐵盆，這是中國人用的「秤」。她們大都會按最接近的，但必定是最重的重量叫價。隨着更多超級市場和店

今天那裏還能找到磨刀師傅嗎？磨刀是一種逐漸式微的服務，假如你廚房裏沒有磨刀石，在一些舊區還能找到不多的師傅提供這種服務。

THE FISH VENDOR
賣魚販

A cry of "maai yue" would announce that the lady had arrived from Aberdeen with fresh fish for sale. Once you had chosen your fish, she would then weigh it on her scales. Not scales as we know them now, but a stick, a piece of string, a

舖開設，街頭叫賣的小販逐漸消失，這種具東方特色的景象也湮沒於社會之中。

這些就是一九五零年代的香港，每天為生活營役的人物。

THE DAI PAI DONG
大排檔

The dai pai dong was a roadside eatery, referred to in English as a cooked food stall. It got its name from the size of its licence, which was bigger than those of other licensed street vendors.

The dai pai dong is a very strong part of the collective memory of Hong Kong people and the green-painted kitchen with its flaming wok can never be forgotten, together with the special and famous milk tea which was only available there.

These unlicensed food stalls first appeared at the end of the nineteenth century and were dotted around Central, Happy Valley, Wong Nai Chong and Wanchai. It was sometime after the war ended in 1945 that the colonial government issued licences to families of injured civil servants and families of the deceased, so that they could earn a living. The stalls provided basic everyday food such as rice, noodles and congee with "yau char kwai" served up in its various forms for those who could not afford more.

One of the unusual features of these cooked stalls was what is known as "cross-stall ordering". Each stall had limited dishes so if someone was eating fried noodles and wanted a cup of milk tea, it could be ordered from another stall, often three or four stalls away, and payment settled later. There were no liquor licences so beer was produced from under the counter in a rice bowl!

As the popularity of these stalls increased, so too did the dishes which began to provide more than just the noodles or rice. For example, there were noodles with chicken giblets, heart and intestine, crispy skin roast goose and rice and even European style sandwiches made with tinned luncheon meat and fried egg.

There were other dishes such as white rice and cha sui or siu mei or Chiu Chow noodles, egg noodles, and rice noodles. They were all available in some form or another. The orders were freshly cooked while one sat on a stool and watched and dodged as the flames shot out in all directions.

Like so many other street vendors who have since disappeared, these dai pai dongs are almost extinct. New licensing laws have meant that most have had to close down for good. It seems that there are now only about twenty-five genuine dai pai dongs still in operation, and those that survive are under cover and are no longer true dai pai dongs.

It was the perfect place for a quick snack at two o'clock in the morning when we gweilos were on our way home from a party joining in the fun and laughter of the locals, who thought we were all mad.

大排檔就是在路邊的餐館，英語指的熟食攤檔，是因為按牌照規定的大小規模，比街頭持牌小販的大而得名。

大牌檔是香港人集體回憶的重要部份，綠色鐵皮搭建的廚房，火光熊熊的鑊氣，以及名聞遐邇，只有它們才售賣的特色港式奶茶，令人難忘！

這些無牌的熟食攤檔最先出現於十九世紀末，分佈於中環，跑馬地，黃泥涌及灣仔。大概到了一九四五年戰爭結束，殖民地政府為了讓那些受傷的公務員家屬和死難者的家屬得以維持生計，遂發牌給他們經營。這些攤檔為條件較差的市民，提供不同款式的日常基本食物如粥，粉，麵，飯和「油炸鬼」。

這些熟食攤檔其中一個特色的地方，就是可以「跨檔點餐」，由於每檔提供的菜式有限，如果你在食炒麵而又想要一杯奶茶，他們通常可以從三，四檔以外的攤檔給你點過來，結帳時才一起算。由於他們沒有酒牌，啤酒就只能偷偷的倒到碗中給你。

隨着大牌檔數目增加和普及，菜式供應不再局限於飯，麵。例如雞雜麵，脆皮燒鵝飯，以至於歐式的午餐肉炒蛋三文治都有。

其他菜式如义燒，燒味飯，潮州河粉，蛋麵和米粉等，都有不同款式供應。餸菜都是下單即煮，坐在櫈子上看着熊熊爐火，鑊氣四溢，但有時卻要閃避四方八面噴出的火 。

像許多已消失的街頭小販一樣，大牌檔也幾乎絕迹。新的發牌條例意味着它們大多要倒閉，今天只剩下約二十五家真正的大牌檔仍在營業，生存的也已遷到室內，不再是真正的大牌檔了。

大牌檔是吃快餐的理想地方，凌晨二時，當我們這群剛參加完派對回家路上的鬼佬，也融入本地人的歡樂與笑聲的時候，他們心想我們定是瘋了。

SWEET BEAN CURD (Dow fu fa)
豆腐花

Soybean has always been an integral part of the Chinese diet, so this "sweet" was a popular item. Because of its soft blancmange constituency, you had to bring your own container in order to take it home for your meal – no polystyrene or plastic bags available then.

The vendor would arrive on his bicycle with a covered wooden tub containing the "dow fu fa" attached to the back. For those who had a sweet tooth he would sprinkle a spoon of brown sugar on top – delicious! This sweet bean curd can still be bought today in a shop or restaurant but no longer from a street vendor.

中國飲食經常有用大豆做食材，用它來造的甜品 — 豆腐花，也非常受歡迎。由於它的結構好像「奶凍」般軟滑，你必需自備容器才能把它帶回家(那時候並沒有膠盒或膠袋)。小販騎着尾部有一個盛着豆腐花的有蓋木桶的單車，在街頭叫賣。假如你是嗜甜的人，他會為你在豆腐花灑上黃糖粉 — 真個美味！今天你仍可在食店或餐館中品嘗到豆腐花，但街頭叫賣的則欠奉了。

STINKY BEAN CURD (Chow dow fu)
臭豆腐

It would not take a strong sense of smell to know that this vendor was close by and that he was very popular. The deep-fried fermented bean curd which gave out this incredibly nasty smell while being cooked on the roadside was sold for ten cents for two triangular pieces wrapped in a piece of paper and topped with chili sauce. The vendor carried his entire shop on the end of a bamboo pole. One end held the box with the stove to heat up the cooking oil for the tofu and on the other end were pieces of paper, toothpicks to stab the fried bean curd, and the chilli. In spite of the smell it really was delicious – if you liked bean curd.

As the years went by, people began to think that having food cooked in the streets was unhygienic, and it probably was, but I seem to have survived it as I am sure many others have too.

就算你的嗅覺不怎麼靈敏，也知道賣臭豆腐的人就在附近，它是當時流行的街頭小食。小販在路邊擺檔售賣，一根大竹杆兩端便挑着他的整家店子；一端的木箱放着炸豆腐的火爐和油鑊，另一端的就是包裝用的紙張，刺著豆腐進食的牙簽和辣醬。發酵的豆腐經油炸釋出令人難以置信的臭味，三角形的豆腐用紙張包住並放上辣醬，兩件僅售一毫。若你喜歡豆腐又能忍受那氣味，它不失為一道美味小食。

隨着時間流逝，人們想到街頭販賣熟食終究不衛生，我不敢否定，但我和其他許多人吃了也無礙。

THE THREADER
線面美容師

One thing that used to fascinate me as a child was watching the removal of women's facial hair by a "threader". This was someone who did not use a razor or tweezers but as the name suggests, thread. The customer would sit on a stool while the threader held one end of a twisted loop of thread in her mouth, and the other in her hands. She then rolled the fine thread up and down the forehead and beyond the natural hairline very fast. It looked very painful to me, but I noticed that the recipient never complained. This would then be followed by the cleaning of the ears.

其中一種東西吸引着我的就是「線面」，無需剃刀，只用一根線就能把女人臉上的汗毛刮淨。顧客坐在木櫈上，線面師傅手拉着線的一端，口咬着另一端；她的那根線就在客人的髮線與前額之間快速上下滾動。我看着也覺得痛楚，但客人卻沒半點投訴，線面完畢接着便是採耳(清潔耳朵)。

THE RATTAN/WICKER SHOP
藤／柳條編織店

Many people confuse the terms rattan and wicker, and think both are materials used for making furniture, baskets,

food trays, etc. In fact, wicker strictly describes the process used: wickerwork. It is a technique rather than a material, although it has also come to be used as a generic name for the materials which are employed, be they rattan, cane, bamboo, or sea grass.

For hundreds of years, rattan has been used by the

Chinese to make many practical items, one of them being hats. Rattan is a tall pole-like vine that grows rapidly in the jungles of Southeast Asia and is a close relative of the palm tree. The outside skin of the rattan stem can be stripped off and is used to bind the joints of furniture together. It is also the material from which the hats are made. When completed, the hats are given a coat of lacquer for waterproofing and thus serve to keep off the rain as well as the sun. Although Chinese hats can also be woven from other materials, the rattan hat is probably the sturdiest.

Three main types of rattan hats were once commonplace in Hong Kong, and they are distinguishable by their differing shapes. The most outstanding and readily recognised is the "Hakka" hat, a flat circular rattan brim with a short black cloth curtain around the edge and a hole in the middle to fit over the crown of the head. Although it is referred to as a "Hakka" hat and worn by women working outdoors, especially in the fields (see right in the picture), it is not only Hakka women who wear them.

However, these hats are never worn by men, who have their own style of rattan hat, which is larger and comes to a point in the middle in a short spike. These are often referred to as coolie or paddy hats (see rear of the picture) and were once commonly worn by men who laboured in the sun. On a hot day, rattan hats could be dipped in water and when put back on the head, served to cool the wearer by the water's evaporation.

The third type of hat is that of the Tanka people. These are the fishing descendants of some of Hong Kong's first settlers who traditionally lived on their boats. This hat also has its own special shape and men and women working on fishing boats and small wooden sampans can still occasionally be seen wearing them. The brim is narrower than the coolie hat and slightly curved, and the crown is deeper; the more compact design is better suited to life on a boat (in the picture, these domed hats are stacked next to the Hakka hats). No longer seen or used is the small round hat the rickshaw coolies wore; and, sadly, as time progresses these others may disappear, too. The shops selling them, and other hand-made rattan items that were once ubiquitous, can only rarely be seen today.

很多人都把藤及柳條這兩個字詞混淆了，以為都是用來製造傢俱，籃及食物盤等的材料。嚴格而言，柳條其實是指製作過程 — 柳條編織，雖然很多材料如藤，蔗，竹及海草的製成品都被通稱為柳條，但它是工藝而非物料。

數百年來，藤一直被中國人用來製造實用品，其中一樣就是帽。藤是一種很高的柱狀藤蔓植物，生長於東南亞森林，生長速度快，是棕櫚樹的近親。藤幹的外皮可以剝下來，用作綑縛家具的接口部位，同時也是製帽的材料。製成帽後，表面髹漆來防水，既可防雨又防曬。雖然中國人的帽還有用其他的物料來編織，但藤可算是最耐用。

在香港較為普遍的藤帽主要有三種，三種形狀各有不同。其中最特出又較為人熟悉的是「客家」帽，它是圓形扁平藤織帽，帽緣周邊垂下短黑紗布簾，中空圓洞供戴在頭頂上。儘管它被稱為「客家」帽，是給那些户外工作的女人穿戴，尤其是下田的(看右圖)，但也不僅是客家女人才戴。

但男人就從不戴這種帽。他們有另一種是圓錐形，體積較大的藤帽，帽心有小尖釘，這些通常稱為苦力或農夫帽（看後圖），一般是給在烈日下勞動的男人穿戴。在熱天的時候，把藤帽泡在水中然後戴上，蒸發帽中的水份可予人涼快的感覺。

第三種是蛋家人戴的帽。他們多是香港原居民，漁民的後代，傳統居住在船上。這種帽有它的獨特形狀，現在仍不時看見在漁船或小艇上工作的男女穿戴。它的帽沿比苦力帽窄及微曲，冠也比較深，緊湊的設計更適合在船上穿戴，（見圖，這些圓拱形的帽堆放在客家帽的旁邊）。但人力車伕戴的小圓帽已不復見，令人傷感的是，隨著時間的流逝，這些不同的帽也可能跟著消失。售賣這些帽子及其他藤編織品的店舖，曾經流行一時，今天也鮮有見到。

WASHING CLOTHES
洗衣服

How would you wash your clothes if you didn't have a washing machine? Of course, by hand in a tub. Not much fun if you have a family of five or more to wash for. That is what had to be done in the late 1940s and 1950s before Hong Kong started to import washing machines. Our amah would sit on a stool with a large wooden tub full of clothes and a washing board. The washing board was also wooden and was cut in ridges all the way down and it was here that she rubbed and scrubbed the clothes until they were almost threadbare but very clean. The advent of the washing machine saved a great deal of hard work and time, but I don't think the clothes were any cleaner.

Likewise, how would you iron your clothes without an electric iron? Across the road from the Peninsula Hotel was the Peninsula Annex on the corner of Middle Road and Nathan Road and in there was the laundry room where all the hotel sheets and linen were taken to be washed and ironed. A strange smell would waft through the door and attracted our attention, so we had to investigate. It was the smell of burning charcoal which the amahs used in the irons to smooth the sheets. These irons were made of cast iron and were very heavy, with the heat emanating from the charcoal burning inside. The laundry had several irons and each one was filled in turn with red-hot charcoal, so the iron stayed hot for as long as the charcoal continued to burn.

如果你沒有洗衣機，你會怎樣洗衣服？當然是用手和木桶。一九四零年代末，五零年初，當洗衣機還沒有進口香港的時候，人們就是這樣洗衣服的了。假如你要洗一家五口的衣服，那真是了無樂趣。我家的女傭坐在櫈子上，面前放着裝有大堆衣服和洗衣板的大木桶。木製的洗衣板表面割成鋸齒狀，衣服放在上面往返磨擦，纖維漸見磨薄，但卻洗得相當潔淨。發明洗衣機省卻大量的勞動力和時間，但衣服不見得洗得更潔淨。

同樣地，沒有電熨斗你會怎樣熨衣服？從半島酒店橫過馬路，在中間道和彌敦道的街角便是半島的

a cheap item that could be bought from any small shop for about twenty cents and the idea of the game was to keep it up in the air by kicking it with the side of the foot and not let it drop to the ground. Sometimes players would see how many times they could keep it going themselves; at other times maybe six or seven would kick it around, usually until it fell apart. It was very cheaply made of a few chicken feathers attached to a base of round cut newspaper. Young people would spend hours kicking these about in the middle of Peking Road, Hankow Road and Middle Road. Cars were few and far between and if one came by there was always time to move out of the way.

加建部份，那裏就是洗衣房，酒店用的枱布和牀單都在這裏洗熨。奇異的氣味從門縫滲出，吸引我去查個究竟，原來這是燒炭的氣味；鑄鐵造的熨斗非常沉重，女傭就是把燒紅的炭放入內加熱熨斗，熨平牀單。洗衣房有多部熨斗，每部都裝滿燒得紅紅的炭，燃燒的炭能維持熨斗的熱力。

PLAYTIME
遊戲時間

During my childhood, there were no purpose-built playing fields or playgrounds in Tsim Sha Tsui, so many young people spent the hot evenings in the street playing various games, one of which was a shuttlecock game. The shuttlecock was

我的孩提時代尖沙咀是沒有休憩公園或遊樂塲的，炎夏的黃昏，年青人只能在街頭玩各式各樣的遊戲，其中一種便是踢毽。毽子構造簡單，以厚厚一叠報紙割成圓形作為底部，幾根雞毛紮在一起插在上面。它價格低廉，只售兩毫一只，很多小店都能買到。玩法就是用腳內側踢在毽子底部，令它停留空中不掉到地上；個人踢毽就是計算毽子被踢起多少次而不會掉到地上；有時會是六，七人圍在一起踢毽互傳，直到毽子掉到地上為止。他們多在北京道，漢口道和中間道街頭圍着踢毽，一踢便是個多小時。但不用擔心，那個年頭的街道車輛稀疏，偶有車輛駛經也有足夠時間避開。

DAIRY FARM ICE CREAM
牛奶公司雪糕

The Dairy Farm popsi man, as we called him, went around the streets on his bicycle selling ice cream in tubs and popsicles of different flavours. He had a covered box on the front of the bicycle which held huge chunks of ice to keep his goods from melting. He would wait outside the school at break and lunchtime, selling ice cream tubs for thirty cents each and the popsi for ten cents each. I think it was the only time in my life that I saw a double popsi, which was twenty cents and had two sticks. The bright green lime-flavoured popsi was my favourite but there were other good flavours too, including one made from milk.

踏着單車穿梭大街小巷，售賣裝在箱內的雪糕和不同味道的雪條，我們稱他為牛奶公司「雪條佬」。單車前頭放着裝有冰塊的有蓋箱子，防止雪糕，雪條溶化，每逢小息便在校外等候我們光顧。雪糕每杯售三毫，雪條每根一毫。這是生平唯一一次看見「孖條」— 兩根木棒的雪條，售價兩毫。我的至愛是鮮綠色的青檸味道，還有其它味道，包括一款牛奶製成的。

SPITTOONS
痰罐

One thing that I was not sorry to say goodbye to was the spittoon. No one really seems to know why such an unhealthy item was introduced into restaurants and public places, especially as tuberculosis was very prevalent after the war. They were made of brightly coloured enamel and resembled the potties used by children. Maybe the spittoon was better than the floor. It is not something I wish to elaborate on, but I can say that the inhuman noise made prior to the expulsion of sputum was quite disgusting, especially if you were at one of the adjacent tables trying to eat!

有一樣東西是我毫不惋惜說再見的就是痰罐。沒有人明白為什麼要在餐館或公眾地方，放一個這樣不衛生的東西，特別是戰後肺癆病流行。痰罐都是用色彩鮮艷的搪瓷製成，與小孩的便壺十分相似。可能吐到痰罐總比地上好，對此我不想多着筆墨，皆因面對它吐痰的呼吐聲委實令人厭惡，尤其是它就放在你的餐桌旁！

ERADICATING RATS
滅鼠

War brings all sorts of nasty things, not the least rats; and because of the lack of public works during the war they increased by the thousands. They were everywhere. In the back streets, in hotels, in restaurants, and in people's homes. If you were able to catch them dead or alive, you could take them down the road to the nearest lamp post to which a box was attached and marked RATS. They would be disposed of by the Public Works Department, but it took many years of effort before the rat population had visibly decreased.

戰爭帶來各種令人討厭的東西，老鼠便是其中之一，由於戰時缺乏市政服務，數量以千計增長。牠們無處不在，後巷，酒店，餐館，以及人們的家中。如果你能活捉或殺死牠們，你可以把牠們放進掛在街上燈柱寫有「老鼠」的箱內，工務司署的工人會清理牠們。經過多年的努力，目測老鼠的數量有所減少。

KAI TAK AIRPORT
啟德機場

When I left Hong Kong in 1952 to go to boarding school in the United Kingdom, we flew in a British Overseas Airways Corporation (BOAC, now British Airways) plane with a propeller engine which took three days to get there. We made an overnight stop staying at the Bluebird hotel in Karachi, by then already part of Pakistan, while the plane was completely serviced and refuelled.

Before boarding the plane, not only was our luggage weighed but so were we, and the officials were meticulous in making sure that each person's allowance was not an ounce over the limit. My friends came to see me off and stood at the wire fence to say goodbye as my mother and I walked out to the plane, which was no more than fifty yards away. Once we were on board and the plane began to move, the traffic was held up while we taxied across the main road and the pilot turned the plane around. While the plane was stationary, the engines were revved to full power twice and on the third time we gathered speed, tore down the runway, and took off. Sitting by the window at night I noticed flames spewing out from the engines but was told by the hostess not to be concerned because it was quite normal and could only be seen at night, although it was still happening during daylight.

Thinking about it today, I can't help wondering how dangerous that must have been.

一九五二年，我離港赴英國入讀寄宿學校，乘坐的就是英國海外航空公司（英國航空公司前身）的螺旋槳飛機，途中需在卡拉奇的藍鳥酒店住一個晚上，她當時已是巴基斯坦一部份，飛機在那裏進行檢查及加油，三天才能到達。

登機前，行李和乘客都必須過磅，工作人員認真地確保每位乘客和行李都不能超重。朋友們隔着鐵絲網圍欄跟我道別，母親陪着我走到五十碼外的飛機登機。所有人登機後，飛機隨即啟動，滑行橫過馬路並準備調頭，兩邊來往的車輛都被截停，好讓飛機走過。飛機進入跑道後停下來，引擎全速加速兩次，第三次起動即全速前進，凌空跑道，一飛沖天。晚上我憑窗外望，注意到引擎噴出火花，機艙服務員告訴我這屬正常，只有晚上才能看見，但實情是白天也有出現。

今天回想起來，我其實是身處險境！

BIRDS
雀鳥

Hong Kong has always been on the migration route for birds going north to south and vice versa, stopping off at the Mai Po Marshes and what existed of Lau Fau Shan out in the New Territories. But if the weather was bad, these birds sometimes got blown off course and very often landed up in Tsim Sha Tsui. There were no tall buildings in the area at the time and the birds would land on the roofs of the houses along Hanoi Road, Humphreys Avenue and Mody Road, as well as the Kowloon Cricket Club in Cox's Road.

One of the most amazing sights I have ever seen in Hong Kong was the arrival of a migrating flock of geese.

One morning I met a friend somewhere near the Kowloon Cricket Club. As we approached the club, the chatter and calling of the birds got louder and louder and there sitting on the roof of the clubhouse and covering the entire cricket field were hundreds of geese all having their say. The birds

were grey in colour with a black head, but I have no idea what geese they were. Several species are known to visit Hong Kong, if not on a regular basis. Unfortunately, I had no camera. The scene would certainly have made an unusual photograph.

It was a most unforgettable sight: indelibly printed in my mind, but never to be seen again.

香港向來是候鳥南北往返的中途棲息地，牠們大都停留在新界流浮山附近的米埔濕地。但假如天氣欠佳而迷途，尖沙嘴通常就是牠們的落腳點。記得當時還沒有高樓大廈，雀鳥一般會棲息在河內道，堪富利士道，麼地道一帶建築物屋頂，和覺士道九龍木球會。我在香港所見過最令我嘖嘖稱奇的一幕，就是這許候鳥的駕臨。

一天早上，我在九龍木球會附近踫到一位朋友，當我們步向球會，聚集那裏的鵝叫聲越來越大，牠們有的站在會所屋頂，但數以百計更多的鵝佈滿整個木球場，爭相向我們高聲打招呼。牠們黑頭灰色鵝身，但緣何聚集這裏，確實令人費解！可惜的是當時我沒有照相機，否則一幀罕見的照片，便能流傳下來。

這是難忘的一幕，烙在心坎中不能磨滅，只此一次不復見。

PEKING ROAD MARKET
北京道街市

Right in the heart of Tsim Sha Tsui, on the corner of Peking Road and Canton Road, was a large food market that catered to most of Kowloon's residents. It was the only one for miles around. The market and surrounding streets were typical of the time, full of rubbish, dirty, rat-infested and always busy.

There were stalls with dried fish covered in flies, every type of offal you can name, "thousand-year-old eggs" in large jars, live chickens and ducks in wicker baskets, as well as melons, green leafy vegetables and fruit. Large opened sacks of rice were lined up along the edge of the pavement and also bags of bright red melon seeds. It was all under one roof and very cheap compared with prices of today. Eggs were twenty

cents each and watermelons (which we were not allowed to eat because of cholera) one dollar each or twenty cents for a slice. And above all, there were no plastic bags… Shoppers used rattan baskets or carried a fish home hanging on a piece of raffia. It was of its time.

座落在尖沙嘴市中心，北京道和廣東道交界，就是方圓數哩內唯一的大型街市，主要是服務九龍區的居民。 街市和周圍的街道都是昔日的典型 — 滿佈垃圾，骯髒，老鼠出沒和經常繁忙。

售賣滿佈蒼蠅的鹹魚的攤檔，你所熟識的各種內臟，大缸裝着的「千年蛋」－皮蛋，關在柳條藤籠裏的活雞，鴨，還有各樣的瓜，菜和水果。大麻包袋裝着的大米和一袋袋的紅瓜子，排列在行人路旁。售賣的食品包羅萬有，價錢和今天相比真有天壤之別！雞蛋兩毫一只，西瓜一元一個(由於霍亂的緣故，父母不讓我進食) 或兩毫一塊。還有的是那時候沒有膠袋，人們買餸都是拿着舊式藤籃，或是用一根水草綑着一條魚帶回家；這就是昔日的境況。

MOTOR BUSES
巴士

In 1947 the Kowloon Motor Bus Company (founded in 1933) took delivery of fifty single-decker buses from England to replace the modified trucks which were initially brought into service after the war. These buses had a door at each end of the vehicle and either could be used by passengers to get on or off, which as you can imagine caused a lot of pushing and shoving. There was no such thing as queuing in those days and this really caused a free for all. If you weren't careful, you could be the first at the bus stop but never get on the bus! Along the length of the bus, inside the roof, was a long cord which passengers pulled to ring the bell: once to stop the bus, and the conductor would ring twice to let the driver know he could go.

Children paid ten cents and adults twenty cents. The conductor collected the money and gave out a punched ticket. Often the bus was so full that he was unable to push his way down the aisle, so he would get off at a bus stop, collect the fares through the window and get back in at the other end. I am sure many people got a free ride on a regular basis. Needless to say, the buses were hot, stuffy and smelly during the summer months.

The main Kowloon terminus was right by the Star Ferry,

where it still stands today. Remarkably, I still use the number 7 bus to the Star Ferry, which I have done for the past seventy and more years.

Another bus I often took, to go swimming at the United Services Recreation Club, was the route 10, which operated from the Star Ferry to the Monument. I got off at its terminus at the junction of Jordan Road and Gascoigne Road adjacent to the Diocesan Girls' School, where stood a very tall obelisk. It was a local landmark, but as a child it never occurred to me to ask what it was a monument to. Before long, it had gone, removed to the colonial cemetery in Happy Valley to make way for development.

In fact, it was a granite memorial to five French sailors who died on the *Fronde* in the calamitous typhoon of 1906 in which more than 10,000 people in Hong Kong lost their lives, most of them fishermen. The typhoon came and went with ferocious force and speed, the limitations of meteorology at the time making it impossible to forecast.

The *Fronde* was a well-built ocean-going destroyer and it ended up stranded and half-submerged on the shores of Kowloon. One can only imagine what happened to the wooden craft of the fisherfolk.

一九四七年，九龍巴士公司(成立於1933)從英國添置了五十輛單層巴士，代替那些由卡車改裝，戰後投入服務的巴士。這些巴士的兩端都有門供乘客上落，你可想像這樣的情況下，少不免會出現擁擠和造成推撞。昔日的乘客沒有排隊的習慣，你一個不留神，可能是第一位到站頭，但卻是永遠擠不上巴士。沿着長長的巴士頂部有一根

長繩，乘客拉一下繩子响鈴要求下車，售票員則拉兩下示意可開行。票價成人兩毫，小童一毫；售票員收費後會發給你一張打孔的車票。有時候車廂太擁擠，售票員無法走向乘客收費，他會等待下一站停車時走下車，從窗口向裏面的乘客收費，基於此我肯定很多人都曾經有乘搭免費巴士。不用多講，夏天的巴士車廂內是炎熱，擠逼和充滿汗水氣味。

九龍區的主要巴士總站就在天星碼頭旁邊，今天仍舊在那裡。值得一提的是我仍乘坐7號巴士到天星碼頭，過去七十多年如是。

另一條我經常乘坐前往三軍會游泳的巴士線就是10號，它來往天星碼頭到紀念碑。我就在佐敦道與加士居道交界，毗鄰拔萃女書院的總站下車，那裏矗立着一座很高的尖方形紀念碑，它是當時的地標，那時是小孩的我，從沒想過要知道這是一座什麼紀念碑。它沒多久就被移到跑馬地殖民地墳場，騰出地方來發展。

實際上這座花崗岩紀念碑是紀念五名海軍驅逐艦「投石號」上的法國籍船員，他們在一九零六年香港一塲災難性風災中罹難。這塲風災奪去了超過一萬人的性命，大部份是漁民。颱風來勢洶洶且風力猛烈，以當時有限的氣象學知識，實不可能作出預測。

「投石號」是一艘建造優良的遠洋驅逐艦，最終擱淺半沉於九龍岸邊；大家可以想像那些漁民的木船會是什麼下塲。

ACKNOWLEDGEMENTS

銘謝

My grateful thanks to Echo Xu Ning of Shanghai for her help with the initial translation of my script into Chinese. And to Gordon Ng Chun Nam who meticulously read over the English version and translated it into a more local Hong Kong style of writing, my sincere thanks.

Many hours were spent discussing and perfecting the Chinese customs with Vicky M. Sung and I am most grateful for her help and suggestions with some of the details.

Also, my thanks to Brian Eastman (a childhood friend) who contributed the odd little anecdote included here.

My very special thanks to Carol Dyer, my editor, who was always available and who patiently went through my original script with a fine-tooth comb.

Without their help it would have been impossible to have completed the book.

感謝上海的Echo Xu Ning女士為我的初稿提供中文翻譯。衷心感謝Gordon Ng Chun Nam先生認真的閱讀我的英文版本,並將它翻譯成具香港地道色彩的中文版本。

非常感謝Vicky M. Sung女士的幫助,她花了很多時間和我討論及完善了我對中國習俗的了解,並提供了詳盡的意見。

此外,我要多謝「兒時好友」Brian Eastman先生,他為這書貢獻了一些奇聞趣事

我要特別感謝我的編輯Carol Dyer女士,她不但隨傳隨到,還耐心詳閱我的原稿並將之細緻梳理。

沒有她/他們的協助,這書是不可能與大家見面。

Acknowledgement is also made of the following sources – 同時銘謝以下的資料來源

Augustin, Andreas, *The Most Famous Hotels in the World: The Peninsula*, Augustin, 1991.

Cheng Po-hung and Toong Po-ming, *A Century of Kowloon Roads and Streets*. Translated by Irene Cheng, Ko Tim-keung and Paul Levine, Joint Publishing (Hong Kong) Co. Ltd, 2003.

Crisswell, Colin (auth.) and Briggs, Tom (illus.), *Hong Kong: The Vanishing City*, South China Morning Post, 1977.

Wiltshire, Trea, *Hong Kong Pages from the Past*, Formasia Books Ltd, 2003.

Hong Kong: An Impossible Journey through History, Serasia Ltd, 1971.

EXPLORE ASIA WITH BLACKSMITH BOOKS

From bookstores around the world or from *www.blacksmithbooks.com*